Copyright and
Intellectual Property

Copyright and Intellectual Property

by Julius J. Marke

Fund for the Advancement of Education

January, 1967
Library of Congress Catalog Card Number 67-16991
Additional copies of this report are available
without cost from the offices of
The Fund for the Advancement of Education,
477 Madison Avenue, New York, New York 10022.

Editor: Renata von Stoephasius

Design: Gene Paul Muzio

Printing: The Georgian Press, Inc.

CONTENTS

Introduction

The creation and dissemination of intellectual property have become a matter of increasing concern to the civilized world. In recent years particularly, the problems associated with intellectual property and how to protect it have become ever more complex. Scholars are constantly creating new knowledge and systems to further the understanding of our physical and social environment, and more often than not the work is done in collaboration with other scholars.

Two forces have had a profound influence on the development and distribution of scholarly materials: the federal government as a major source of funds, and the growth of reprography with the subsequent vast use of photocopied materials.

The federal government annually grants large sums of money for the development of knowledge, and scholarly research has, to a great extent, come to depend on the government for support. What happens to a scholar's rights of ownership when the materials that he developed were supported by public funds? What is the public interest in this instance? How can it best be served? What are the rights of copyright holders and publishers in relation to government-sponsored projects? Questions such as these are increasingly being raised and debated in the intellectual community as well as before Congress.

Prior to the development of sophisticated photocopying devices that reproduce copies inexpensively, copying was a matter of concern to a few. Now, in this age of the knowledge explosion, it has become a matter of concern to almost everyone involved in education and the development and distribution of intellectual material.

One particular event that helped to bring the problem of ownership of intellectual property into the public arena was the establishment of the public domain policy by the United States Office of Education in 1965. The policy declared, in effect, that materials produced as a result of research activities which had been supported by funds from the Office of Education would be placed in the public domain. The range of materials included writings, recordings, pictures, drawings, graphic presentations, computer programs–virtually every kind of educational material imaginable.

The ruling was intended to make research findings available to the public, quickly and with a minimum of restrictions. Public reaction to this new policy was generally mixed. Some acclaimed it, others denounced it. Some argued that it would expedite the flow of new knowledge; others claimed it would inhibit research. And the controversy continues unabated, with authors, scholars, publishers, government officials, businessmen, educators–and the world of law–discussing its advantages and disadvantages.

It was this policy and the reactions to it that first attracted the staff of the Fund for the Advancement of Education to the problems associated with intellectual property, government-financed research, and a new technology. Clearly, here was an instance where a responsible philanthropic organization, dedicated to the advancement of education, could help by spelling out some of the issues involved in the controversy and suggesting some ways and means to solve them.

In April, 1966, therefore, the Fund's board of directors authorized a study of the public domain issue as raised by the Office of Education policy, fully aware that such a study would also have to touch upon related matters, such as government-financed research and its accessibility, and copyright and reprography.

A month later the Fund engaged Julius J. Marke, professor of law and law librarian at New York University, to conduct such a study. Professor Marke, who is a lawyer, teacher, author, and librarian, brought to his task a rare combination of talents. He represented the American Association of Law Librarians on the Joint Libraries Committee on Fair Use in Photocopying from 1959 to 1962, and is at present a member of the publishing council of the New York University Press. He is the author of *Vignettes of Legal History* and co-editor of the *International Seminar on Constitutional Review.*

Professor Marke, in writing this report, has examined a great number of publications, statements, and opinions, and interviewed more than a hundred persons, each of whom has been or is directly involved with the problems. He has outlined the issue clearly; he has stated and weighed a variety of viewpoints on the public domain question in particular, and related questions in general. He has made some specific recommendations in the public domain area and some general ones in the field of information accessibility, reprography, and the protection of intellectual property. He has also investigated such topics as copyright and technology, and information as a commodity. In all cases the views expressed are Professor Marke's and not those of the Fund for the Advancement of Education.

EDWARD J. MEADE, JR.

Government-Financed Research and Public Domain Policy

A Statement of Policy of the U.S. Office of Education, published in the *Federal Register* of July 28, 1965,[1] has evoked an acrimonious controversy concerning government-supported research and the public domain. The Statement of Policy declared:

> Material produced as a result of any research activity undertaken with any financial assistance through contract with or project grant from the Office of Education will be placed in the public domain. Materials so released will be available to conventional outlets of the private sector for their use.
>
> This policy is effective immediately.
>
> Dated: July 12, 1965
>
> (sgd.) Francis Keppel
> U.S. Commissioner of Education

To implement this new policy, the Office of Education announced that it would insert the following contract language into all new contract instruments and in as many currently effective instruments as could be amended by mutual agreement:

> RELEASE OF MATERIALS TO THE PUBLIC DOMAIN
>
> The term 'materials' as used herein includes all materials, such as writings, sound recordings, pictorial reproductions, drawings or other graphical representations, computer programs, and works of any similar nature specified to be delivered under this contract.
>
> All materials produced under this contract will be placed in the public domain as expeditiously as possible. The contractor agrees not to establish any claim to statutory copyright in the materials. This paragraph is not in any way to be construed as restricting the rights of the contractor to use and/or publish the results of its work. . . .
>
> APPLICABLE TO CURRICULUM DEVELOPMENT RESEARCH ONLY
>
> The contractor and the contracting officer will mutually agree to final dissemination arrangements as an allowable cost to the contract.

Shortly thereafter, officials of the Office of Education explained that their primary purpose in adopting this new policy was to assure competition in the production and dissemination of different versions of curricular materials. They cautioned, however, that "writings" covered scholarly research works as well as monographs that resulted from OE-financed research, and that these also would be affected by the new policy.

Commenting on this new policy at a conference held with representatives of education organizations, Henry Loomis, then Deputy Commissioner of Education, stated: "We want to make this material available to the maximum number of people, in the shortest time, with a minimum of restrictions." Therefore, instead of permitting the contractors and grantees to copyright their government-financed products, the OE would consider subsidizing the publication and dissemination of these products if commercial publishers refused to print and distribute them.

In order to achieve the earliest possible release and publication of these materials without copyright protection, agency officials explained, the new OE contracts would provide that the public domain policy was not to be construed as restricting the rights of the contractor to use and/or publish the results of his work. This new clause superseded the old contract language, which had provided for approval by the OE before the contractor released the results of his work for publication.

The reaction to this new policy by representatives of educational organizations and by publishers was one of strong protest and critical denunciation. Instead of encouraging the publication of research findings, they argued, this would inhibit it. However, certain members of Congress, government officials, and interested persons in the private sector enthusiastically supported the new policy.

The issues of government support of research as it relates to the public domain policy and to the accessibility of government-developed information were thus projected into wide-open examination and debate. For, although the new public domain policy was restricted to the Office of Education, other federal grant-making agencies also began to review their policies in this area. To understand the significance of this highly controversial issue, it is necessary to consider its background and the arguments and proposals of the protagonists involved.

Don K. Price, commenting on government-sponsored research in *Government and Science,* noted the context in which policy decisions thereon are being drawn:

"As it becomes more and more obvious that the research and development of today will determine tomorrow not only the security of the nation, but also the fate of major industries, it is inevitable that the system for the support of research will be drawn more and more into the arena of political controversy. It is even more certain that political critics will become more and more alert to possible cases of conflict of interest–cases in which those whose institutions are supported by government funds have an opportunity to influence the distribution of funds and the determination of policies.

"Such issues will no doubt come up in their most controversial form in industry. Nevertheless they are also likely to come up in the academic world."[2]

The big question is not only who will make the policy decisions regarding government support of research, but how will the public interest best be served by the use of government research funds. An awareness, therefore, of the significance of these research grants and contracts in the development of our society is important.

The growth of the federal government's involvement in research is attested to by the fact that since 1961 it has more than doubled its support, with R. and D. expenditures in fiscal 1966 expected to reach $17 billion, or roughly 15 percent of the total federal budget.

Richard J. Barber, in *The Politics of Research,* reviewed these figures and estimated that 80 percent of the research funds has been paid to non-government contractors in industry, to universities and colleges, as well as to diverse non-profit institutions. These funds have provided direct or indirect support for about two-thirds of this country's skilled scientific personnel. Many institutions of higher learning depend on government research contracts for sizable portions of their budgets.[3]

These statistics indicate that the federal government is playing a dominant role in research and development in the U.S. In fact, it has been suggested by Barber that, in light of this support, domestic research has in a very real sense been "nationalized." "Private industry, diverse non-profit institutions and the colleges and universities–all depend on the government to finance the great bulk of their research activity."[4] Any policy decision, therefore, made by a governmental agency that has direct bearing on research and development programs has wide-reaching repercussions.

According to Lowell H. Hattery, professor at the American University, who recently surveyed the policies of federal agencies in regard to book publishing and research, the Office of Education during the past ten years has spent about $100 million to conduct or support educational research. It spent about $10 million in 1966 alone. The research products of the OE assume such commercial forms as "textbooks, curriculum guides, tape recordings, films and even computer programs," i.e., they are tangible items and thus susceptible to mass production and distribution at a profit. Considering that fact as well as a statement in August, 1966, by Representative Adam Clayton Powell, chairman of the House Education and Labor Committee, to the effect that $400 million had already been authorized for the purchase of books for elementary and secondary schools alone,[5] it becomes readily apparent that the stakes for commercial publishers are high, and that any policy decision of the OE or any other government agency that deprives the private sector of an opportunity to compete for these materials on the open market will evolve into a cause célèbre. OE's new public domain policy clearly raises the basic question of how public funds should be spent.

Copyright, although it is basically a statutory right given to an author to protect his artistic or literary expressions, is in essence a form of exclusivity for a specified period of time. This right of exclusivity, however, is subject to the Constitutional provision that it promote the progress of science and the arts. Hence, there must be a balancing of equities in which the public welfare will always be considered.

In order to evaluate the effect of a public domain policy on government-sponsored research products, the following questions will have to be answered: To what extent will such a policy stimulate or inhibit the researcher or producer? Will the public benefit or lose by this policy? How will the public interest best be served?

The position of the Office of Education on its new public domain policy has been explained by Walter E. Mylecraine, Special Assistant to the Deputy Commissioner of Education.[6] Under the old policy, he pointed out, researchers working under OE grants or contracts were allowed to copyright their research and the educational materials stemming from it. Generally, the project contract stipulated that the researcher or other contracting party give the government an "irrevocable, royalty-free license to use the work as it chose and to 'authorize others so to do'." As a practical matter, however, this privilege was rarely exercised by the OE "simply because its stewardship of educational research was a relatively minor responsibility."

The basic reason for the change in policy, according to Mylecraine, was a conviction on the part of OE officials that "research produced with public funds should become public property. The benefits incident to expressing this principle in a public domain policy begin with the total elimination of Federal control over research materials. The administrative effect of the policy is to take such materials out of the hands of the Government and turn them over to the public as soon as grants or contract terms have been met. Thus, it is not the Office of Education but the educational market place–publishers, superintendents, school purchasing agents, librarians, and the students themselves – that will evaluate these materials and decide how they can best be used.

"Even more important, we believe the new policy will improve the quality of research supported by the Office of Education. We believe it will foster in educational research generally a creativity, a cooperation, and a competition that copyrighting can tend to discourage. The public domain policy not only permits a scholar to build on the foundation laid by another, but in fact encourages him to do so. He can retain some sections of a published work in their original form and adapt others. . . . The researcher who invests his own time at his own risk to develop an item of educational material has created a piece of private property just as surely as the man who builds his own home with his own funds. But the researcher working under an OE grant or contract is using public funds, and he should no more have a legal monopoly over the fruits of that research than a road builder should own the highway he has built under public contract."

Realizing that the publishers would have adverse reactions to this policy, Mylecraine called their attention to the fact that the Warren Commission report on the assassination of President Kennedy, the Surgeon General's report on smoking and cancer, and the *Statistical Abstract of the U.S.*, all in the public domain, did not deter them from reprinting these books. "Timely marketing and attractive presentation," he feels, "are worthy substitutes for exclusive ownership in profitable publishing."

Mylecraine also commented on the objection of scholars who fear that once their material is in the public domain anyone may modify it or tamper with it as he chooses, so that an author may see some strange versions of his original work. Noting that "no scholar would claim ultimate wisdom," he explained that "the Office of Education not only recognizes that others may adapt to new uses work supported by public funds but in fact hopes they will. The resulting changes may be for the worse as well as for the better . . . such risk is inherent in all innovation, and American education badly, badly needs innovation."

In conclusion, Mylecraine observed that the OE has need for both publishers and scholars, and reiterated its belief "that the production and dissemination of research materials under a public domain policy leave plenty of room for all involved to seek their own varied interests." The new policy, he predicted, will "speed the advance of educational research and encourage the operation of free enterprise mechanisms in educational publishing."

Although Harold Howe II, the present U.S. Commissioner of Education, did not participate in the formulation of the public domain policy, he has expressed his support of it. He agrees with the government's preserving a free position as a third party between consumers and publishers, but he is not certain whether an open policy or a public domain policy is the best way to express this interest. As more and more government money is poured into educational research, the questions of how these publicly supported research materials should be produced and who should have access to them become more important.

The proposition that public investment should not be permitted to result in private franchise or privilege has frequently been voiced and argued by Congressmen and others who have injected themselves into the public domain debate.

Senator Russell B. Long (Louisiana) has been an advocate of the public domain policy for many years, particularly with reference to government-supported research resulting in patentable inventions. He has expressed his position before the Education Subcommittee of the Senate's Labor and Public Welfare Committee.[7]

Stressing that section 8 of the copyright law expressly provides that "no copyright shall subsist in any publication of the U.S. government or any reprint in whole or in part thereof," he maintained that "the original and continuing purpose of this prohibition is to assure maximum availability and dissemination of informational material prepared by or for the government at the expense of the public. . . . Knowledge developed by contractors and grantees at great public expense should also be freely available to the press, to scholars, to private enterprise, and to the public at large. Since federal outlays for research now total over $15 billion annually, this matter is of far-reaching importance.

"The basic question involved is whether research financed by the government should be subject to copyright control . . . or should such research be freely accessible to all segments of our society.

"The present practices of many government agencies permit research contractors and grantees to sell exclusive publishing rights to the fruits of publicly financed research. This in my judgment is contrary to the public interest."

Refuting as "patently fallacious" the publishers' claim that "prohibition of copyright restrictions over government-financed material will discourage private publications and thereby reduce public accessibility of such material," he pointed to the wide publicity given by professional journals, newspapers, and popular magazines to non-copyrightable statements by government officials, papers by government scientists, and reports by government agencies. Publishers have claimed that much of the government-supported material is of such limited interest that private publication is not feasible unless they are granted copyright protection, to which Senator Long responded that, if the market were so small, why should a publisher fear competition from another publisher? "Would not the second publisher know that he could not make a profit since someone else had preempted the market? Wouldn't the very fact of a limited market protect the initial publisher of government research?" To contend that the publications of the Government Printing Office have small distribution and promotion, he feels, is ridiculous. Many of them are sold in millions of copies and "the 'limited audience' argument fails both in logic and experience."

Commenting on one publisher's argument that publication by the government costs the taxpayer money which could be saved if research works were issued privately under copyright, the Senator notes that many government publications are self-supporting and that the Superintendent of Documents has been operating at a profit. It appears, he said, that "what the publishers are seeking is privileged monopolies, denying the public access to what it already paid for unless it makes an additional payment to the publisher who happened to secure the copyright. They argue that the federal government should both finance the research and protect private profit in its publication through a copyright monopoly. This is tantamount to saying that the government should finance the building of highways and then permit private companies to charge tolls."

Senator Long feels so strongly about the public domain issue that he has from time to time proposed amendments that would prohibit the patenting of discoveries that have resulted from federal research and development expenditures in the field of science and technology. These amendments have been proposed for the Water Resources Research Act of 1964, the Coal Research Act, the Helium Act, the Saline Water Act, the disarmament research bill, and the Mass Transit Act of 1964. Since 1965 these "Long amendments," as they are called, have been expanded to include copyright, and have been added to the water-pollution bill as well as to the Appalachian Region Development Act of 1965. They provide for copyrighting of materials resulting in whole or in part from government R. and D. contracts and grants in countries other than the U.S., but in this country they give a blanket license to anyone who wants to reproduce and use the materials. Similar amendments will be proposed by Senator Long to bills involving medical research, medical libraries, and health research facilities. He also announced that he plans to offer his amendment to every bill that authorizes research and development grants in the fields of science and technology. In brief, Senator Long sees a copyright as analogous to a patent—a concept with which the publishers are in complete disagreement.

Senators Saltonstall and McClellan have also introduced bills in Congress that prescribe a national policy with respect to patentability of government-financed R. and D. inventions, except that theirs is a more flexible approach, generally permitting the contractor to take title to the invention.[8]

Proponents of the Long amendment see it as an attempt to establish a policy similar to that in effect in industry. A company that finances a research project takes title to any patentable discoveries arising from it. Why should it not be the same when the project has been financed by the American taxpayer? Putting these discoveries in the public domain, they argue, ensures a competitive environment for their marketing and benefits the public through lower prices. This system has been followed for several years by such government agencies as the Department of Agriculture, the Tennessee Valley Authority, and others, where it has worked effectively. Many companies have secured licenses from these agencies and marketed the products at reasonable prices.

Proponents of the public domain policy also raise another disturbing problem, namely that of access to public information. When information is gathered and disseminated by a government agency with or without the help of the private sector, the question arises whether it is public information, and whether the public has a right to know about it. As Robert U. Brown, publisher and editor of *Editor and Publisher,* said in an editorial in that magazine: "The method of classifying government material has supplied government agencies with an excuse to withhold information on the grounds of security—a word that has been abused in many instances. If these same agencies are given the authority to copyright material, the way will be open for discrimination on who can and who cannot publish or reprint what should be public information available to all on equal terms. Exceptions will breed further exceptions, just as censorship begets more censorship. . . ."[9]

Another point should be noted. M. B. Schnapper, editor of the Public Affairs Press and a militant advocate of the public's right to know, believes it is "exceedingly significant that the profits derived from copyrighting of materials prepared at the taxpayer's expense are based largely on royalties paid by public entities–local, state and national (including schools, libraries and government agencies). In effect, the public pays a double subsidy for the privilege of access to public property transformed into private property."[10]

Government-sponsored research involves more than the expenditure of public funds. From management's point of view, the company or institution contracting with the government to engage in this research is making a contribution without which the successful use of public funds would be doubtful. As Don K. Price says in *Government and Science:* "The company is putting at the government's disposal a vast accumulation of expertise and the managerial assets of a going concern–qualities that the government could not possibly provide for itself–and all at the risk that a change in government policy will leave the company in a poor competitive position in its traditional commercial fields. The contractual system has certainly given the government . . . great advantages of flexibility, and it has enabled [it] to make use of managerial talent that under present conditions cannot be found in adequate quantity in government agencies. . . ."[11]

It is significant that the private sector, in trying to recommend criteria for a public domain policy, cannot come to an agreement within its own factions. Basically, commercial publishers agree with Curtis G. Benjamin, chairman of McGraw-Hill Co., that "this USOE policy is needlessly absolute and restrictive and that its observance will be hurtful to governmental, public and publishing interests, [and] that it [should] be carefully reconsidered." They also agree that "other federal departments and agencies [should] . . . take a broad and flexible view of the matter, with due regard for precedents and practices under which hundreds of government-financed works have been commercially published with benefit to everyone involved."

Publishers further agree that most government publications could be classified in one of four categories and that "the problems of private copyright, government property, and the public interest vary somewhat with respect to each category."[12]

Benjamin lists the four categories as follows:

1. Reports of *ad hoc* commissions, committees, task forces, delegations, symposia, etc.

2. Works written or edited "for hire" (under a federal contract, grant or commission), such as histories, treatises, operating manuals, handbooks, compilations, etc.

3. Reports on research done by non-government personnel under federal contract or grant.

4. Textbooks and associated instructional materials written by contract or grant.

The publishers generally endorse Benjamin's conclusion that in the first three categories the interests of the government and the general public were best served when commercial publication was arranged, for these reasons: 1) The cost of government publication has usually been saved. 2) The work has appeared in a better form with professional editing in the publishing house. 3) Dissemination has been wider than it could have been with only a GPO printing. 4) The work receives more publicity and public recognition, and it is placed more quickly and effectively in the proper literary channels in its field. 5) The specially interested public has paid no more than a fair price for the product.

A large majority of these reports, Benjamin finds, are of such specialized interest and such transient value that it would be unprofitable for more than one publisher to print them. "Two editions issued by two publishers would be profitless; three editions would be ruinous. So with every publisher free to publish such a work, no one actually would." Then, under those circumstances, there should be a GPO printing, but if the GPO publishes a report, the results generally are not as satisfactory as when the private sector prints it. Benjamin also points out that private publications are more apt to be reviewed in professional journals and media other than GPO publications, which are seldom catalogued by libraries in the usual way and are often allowed to go out of print when the first printing is exhausted.

On occasion, Benjamin admits, the government has issued a report of great interest and attraction that has been profitable for several publishers as well as the GPO to publish simultaneously. (The report of the Warren Commission is an example of this type.) "But," he cautions, "for every government report having such wide interest, there are produced at least 200 to 300 that can be published profitably in one edition only." And of course, if the GPO fails to publish these kinds of reports and the publishers refuse because copyright cannot be obtained, there is no dissemination. (The failure of the Office of Education to arrange for a commercial publication of the *Educational Media Index* is a recent case in point.)

Benjamin stated that commercial publication of government-sponsored reports by professional writers and editors, working under a federal contract or grant, is advantageous for the government for these reasons also: The government often receives free copies of the commercial edition for its own use and/or royalty payments, which offset a good part of its expense in the venture; the prospect of private income to the author allows the government to negotiate more advantageous terms in the writing contract; and the prospect of commercial publication under a recognized imprint attracts writers of higher caliber.

What is important, according to Benjamin, is that "private publication of research reports in no way restricts the fullest possible use of research results as reported." Obviously, the publisher has everything to gain by selling the copyrighted version and under the principles of fair use the ideas and contents of the report would be available to all concerned with the research.

Benjamin's views on the desirability of copyrighting government-sponsored research reports reflect in the main the attitude of the private sector. In essence, what the private sector seeks is a more flexible policy in which every federal agency would decide independently whether the situation warranted commercial publication under the terms of the grant or contract. This also coincides with the view of the Register of Copyrights as expressed in his report to Congress on the proposed copyright-law revision:

"Under the definition in section 105(b) there should be nothing to prohibit an independent contractor or grantee from securing copyright in works prepared by him under a government contract or grant, as long as the contract or grant permits it. We believe it is important to preserve the basic right of private authors to secure copyright in these situations, and that any cases in which it is considered desirable to deny or limit protection should be dealt with by agency regulation or contractual provisions, or by separate legislation."[13]

Commercial publishers generally accept the Register's proposal that a government official or employee should "not be prohibited from obtaining copyright protection for any work he produces in his private capacity outside the scope of his official duties."

The American Council of Learned Societies, a primary research contractor for the OE and an association of many scholarly organizations, has also taken a strong stand in support of copyrightability. In a statement presented during the hearings on the proposed copyright-law revision, it stated:

"In defining works of the United States Government, so as to provide that such works are not copyrightable, the revision bill properly excludes from the definition works prepared by universities, other private institutions or individual scholars financed by research grants from the government (sec. 105). The considerations supporting unfettered dissemination of writings by government officers or employees prepared within the scope of their official duties, reflected in the policy decision that such writings should not be copyrightable by the government (or the individuals involved), are not generally applicable to works written by private persons or institutions. These works, produced under various types of government grants in large numbers, do not necessarily deal with subjects of specific governmental concern, but advance knowledge generally. The extent of the economic support afforded by the government grant varies greatly from case to case.

"The investment necessary for publication under private auspices may be impossible to secure without copyright protection, so that denial of copyright may have the effect of narrowing rather than broadening the dissemination of the product of the research grant. In appropriate cases, moreover, the government by agreement with the recipient may take an assignment of the copyright or certain pecuniary or other rights under it (sec. 105 (a))."[14]

Some representatives of educational associations have denounced the OE public domain policy as a policy that will actually inhibit publication. They fear that materials likely to have a limited market may go unpublished if they cannot be protected by copyright. They are also concerned that the quality of research reports may decline if they are arbitrarily placed in the public domain. Some believe that if this policy spreads to other government agencies, the whole question of the participation of scholars in government-sponsored research will be at stake.[15]

The position taken by Senator Long has been attacked by W. Bradford Wiley, representing the American Textbook Publishers Institute as well as the American Book Publishers Council,[16] on the grounds that the Long amendment will have the following effects on the publication of federally supported research and development results: 1) It will reduce the publication of research results and thus limit dissemination; 2) it will increase the cost to the government of whatever dissemination is made; 3) it will tend to defeat the purpose of federal research and development expenditures by limiting the audience to which these results will be made known, and 4) it will transfer publishing activity from the private sector of the economy—both profit and non-profit—to the federal government.

The reason for these results, the publishers contend, is that without copyright protection it will not be economically feasible for them to publish the materials resulting from government-sponsored research. This would be especially true of scientific and technical books, where the market is limited and copies are high priced. Fear of public domain would limit the market even more and prices might go so high as to make an entire project uneconomic. Failure of the private sector to publish such a book might necessitate additional government expenditure in order to publish it through the GPO. As an alternative, the government could subsidize the cost of publishing by a private-sector publisher, or it could distribute typewritten copies of the original report to a few key people.

With reference to Wiley's fourth point, it is of interest to note an observation by Mortimer Caplin, former Commissioner of the Internal Revenue Service: that the problem of government versus business constitutes one of the most pressing problems of our present-day economy.

He recommends that if private industry is doing a reputable job the government should defer to it—even if it can do a better job.

Wiley also made a distinction between patents and copyrights to prove that Senator Long was improperly placing them in the same category in his restrictive amendments. A patent, he maintains, is not analogous to a copyright. "A patent gives its owner an exclusive right to a product or a process. He may use it himself; he may license others to use it, free or at a price; or he may prevent its use by anyone. Thus a patent controls the substance of a new development. A copyright is entirely different in this respect. It requires that the material be published—made available to the public generally. In exchange the author has the right to sell copies or otherwise to control the use of a particular form of expression, but not the substance of the ideas. Thus anything which is published and copyrighted is made available to everyone, and they are completely free to use the information and ideas represented therein."

In connection with GPO publications and its pricing policies, a letter written by James U. Harrison, Public Printer, to Senator Long, and dated March 23, 1965,[17] is enlightening:

"The prices at which government publications are sold by this office [GPO] . . . include, in addition to the cost of printing the extra copies required for sale, a markup sufficient to cover all cost of handling. . . . Because the pricing method established does not include editorial, research, or make-ready costs of the originating government agency, the price of a government edition will probably, in most instances, be lower than that of a comparable commercial issuance. I feel that it is important to recognize that the majority of government publications are small, paperbound pamphlets dealing with highly technical subject matter, which sell for an average of from 15 to 35 cents a copy. While an occasional publication such as the Warren Report, lends itself ideally to commercial reproduction, the same is not true of the thousands of smaller, less popular publications, many of which have contributed so substantially to our progress."

Congressional reaction to the Long amendment has proved to be very interesting. Senator Saltonstall, for example, observed: "...In those instances where the government pays for all research performed under a research and development contract, the government should receive rights to that which is developed under the contract. I believe, however, that [Senator Long] is weak in his argument that disposition of rights under these contracts can be made before a contract is negotiated. It is only when the contract is let that the parties can know what they are entitled to receive.... It is in the national interest to insure that the best qualified sources are used to perform government research and development contracts. If we remove all incentive by providing that no rights of any character shall be given to their inventiveness, we limit the opportunity of the government to establish new facilities and research efforts which will be for the advantage and benefit of all of us...."[18]

Senator Jack Miller objected: "[Senator Pastore] has said that this is a very simple amendment. That is the difficulty with the amendment. It is too simple. It is not just a matter of whether or not we take taxpayers' money and turn it over to a private contractor to be used entirely for research purposes and the contractor does not spend any of his own money. We have no problems with that kind of situation. . . . Are the Senators from Rhode Island and Louisiana willing to say, because the federal government put up $100,000 and the contractor put up $300,000, that it is fair that the whole result should go to the federal government? . . . If the amendment . . . had provided that instead of all the benefits going to the federal government, language something like 'The federal government's fair and equitable share in the information, copyrights, uses, processes, patents, and other developments resulting from the activity will be preserved,' then I think we would have a fair and equitable amendment."[19]

Senator Samuel J. Ervin, Jr. noted during the same colloquy that Senator Long's amendment to the Pollution Bill (S. 4) would discourage local governments from contributing 50 percent of the cost of research projects when the federal government, putting up an equal amount or less, would get exclusive rights to the patents involved.

"Furthermore," he continued, "there are many people with brains who have spent many years of study and research in the purification of water and the elimination of pollution. . . . The Senator's amendment would discourage those people from contributing their brains to research projects in this field, if there is written upon our law books a statute that the federal government would take the benefit of not only the part of the research funds put up by the federal government and private individuals and private industry, but also the benefit of the brains of those people."[20]

It should be noted in this respect that universities provide support for federal research and development grants and contracts in many ways. Reduced teaching schedules and special research funds often represent an impressive contribution to basic research. To such direct allocation can be added a further contribution through absorption of overhead charges that are reimbursed in token amounts by private sources or not fully by numerous federal agencies. The indirect cost of research is often least understood and is of great importance to the financial health of the university. Each program requires space, services, equipment, a library, and other supporting elements.

Broadly speaking, commercial publishers present a united front in favoring copyright protection for government-financed scholarly or scientific works. Scholars, however, have some reservations about the necessity of protecting their right to royalties from these publications, especially when they take the form of articles in professional journals or technical and scientific monographs. Traditionally, scholars are not paid for articles on scientific and technical subjects published by professional journals. If they are paid, the fee is usually nominal and in no way compensatory for the time and secretarial expense involved. Furthermore, the royalties paid for scientific and technical monographs often are not sufficiently large to warrant the expense of accounting for them. Except for these reservations, scholars generally support the publishers' position in this area.

Where government-financed textbooks and associated instructional or curricular materials are concerned, however, the situation changes radically, and the consensus gives way to factionalism.

Government-Financed Curriculum Materials and Public Domain Policy

The government's participation in curriculum reform programs was greatly stimulated by the Russians' launching of Sputnik in the 1950's. The need for improved textbooks and other instructional materials reflecting the new knowledge in mathematics and science had been recognized by responsible educators and scientists before then. But Sputnik became the catalytic agent that propelled the government into action, and aroused tremendous interest in producing new elementary and high school instructional materials for mathematics and science courses. With the great sums of money made available by the government, federally supported curriculum revisions were instituted in physics, mathematics, biology, chemistry, elementary science, earth sciences, foreign languages, and elementary social studies. University scholars and educators were induced to apply their creative imagination and professional experience to the development of these curricula. The results were highly encouraging in some areas, and almost revolutionary in others.[21]

In working out the details for curriculum reform, government agencies usually conformed to a standard operating procedure such as the following:

1. A government agency would contract with a university or other non-profit agency to prepare the curriculum materials. The contracting party was designated a prime contractor.

2. The prime contractor would then arrange to form a curriculum-development team or study group of interested scholars and scientists who would prepare the necessary materials. These scholars were usually members of the faculty of the contracting party. If a non-profit agency other than a university was the contracting party, it would arrange to compensate the members of the team independently by contract.

3. When the materials were finally released by the curriculum-development team, the government agency and/or the prime contractor arranged for commercial publication under competitive bidding. The successful bidder was then permitted to obtain copyright protection of the publication under an arrangement whereby he accounted for royalties to the prime contractor and/or the government agency, depending upon the terms of the initial government grant or contract. Sometimes the contract stipulated that the commercial publisher assign his copyright immediately to the government agency, which then gave him an exclusive license to disseminate the material for a designated number of years.

Although some government officials and prime contractors objected to this arrangement, it was generally accepted as workable and fair. Publishers at first were pleased, for it permitted them to participate in the program without untoward government interference. Later, however, they began to have second thoughts about the advisability of copyrighting these new texts–especially after the copyrighted publication of the Physical Science Study Committee's textbook on physics and its collateral materials, which had been developed under the leadership of Jerrold R. Zacharias, professor at the Massachusetts Institute of Technology. These collateral materials consisted of laboratory guides and apparatus in kit form, more than fifty films that set the tone and standard for the course, achievement tests, an extensive library of paperbound books written by distinguished authors on topics of science, and teacher's guides. The government spent millions of dollars on this project and arranged for promotion and teacher instruction on how to use the PSSC materials in the classroom. The effect on all other physics texts was apparently detrimental, and a strong adverse reaction in the commercial publishing field became noticeable.

For one thing, publishers objected to the dominant position the PSSC text had attained because of the prestige connected with government promotion and sponsorship. This kind of support, they claimed, put all other textbooks in the field at a competitive disadvantage so that nobody would want to introduce new texts. They urged instead that government agencies place all new course and instructional materials produced with federal funds in the public domain so that all publishers would have an equal opportunity to publish their own versions of them.

Presumably, it was this agitation that made the Office of Education decide to place *all* its publications in the public domain. This was more than the publishers had anticipated and they were suddenly confronted with a Frankenstein of their own making. They quickly responded by announcing their support of the public domain policy as long as it was limited to curriculum development materials. They still wanted and actually needed copyright protection for all other scholarly and technical government-financed research reports.

Before considering the various positions taken by the protagonists of the public domain policy on government-financed curriculum materials, it is interesting to note that these materials are published and disseminated differently from other government-supported research reports.

Curtis Benjamin cites these reasons for the differences: 1) Curriculum materials must find their place in a highly competitive market. They must, therefore, be competitively priced yet bear a heavy freight of promotional and teacher-service costs (sample copies for adoption, desk copies after adoption, teachers' manuals, solution manuals, etc., are usually supplied free). 2) These materials involve the commercial publisher in the large professional efforts and high costs required for editorial perfection and classroom testing. Indeed, the publishers' editorial expense is sometimes larger than the government's contribution to the cost of the completed manuscript. Because of this high initial cost, a publisher often does no better than break even on his first edition, and in some cases he suffers a loss. Successful second and third editions must be depended upon for realization of profit.

In testimony before the House Committee on the Judiciary, Lee Deighton, chairman of Macmillan Co., discussed the economics of textbook publishing.[22] Speaking on behalf of the American Textbook Publishers Institute, he stressed that textbook publishing is a "risk enterprise." Schools, he explained, do not buy textbooks on "prospect, they buy only with product in hand." A textbook cannot be market-tested in advance; it finds its way in a competitive market only after it has been produced. "Preparation of manuscripts ranges from an occasional minimum of three years to an occasional maximum of ten years. During this period editorial costs mount and mount. . . . A single high-school textbook will require an investment of $50,000 before the first copy is available for sale. A series of elementary-school textbooks with many components will require as much as a $1 million investment before it is ready for marketing." And despite this risk, "there is no way to know in advance that a book will sell."

Publishers are therefore wary of the implications of a public domain policy that denies them copyright protection, just as they are wary of a policy that denies them a competitive position. And yet, they are divided on whether to support a public domain policy for government-supported textbooks. The ATPI favors a straight public domain policy for government-supported curriculum projects at the elementary and secondary school levels, and is thus basically in agreement with the Office of Education. In its position paper dated February 1, 1965, the institute enthusiastically approved the government's role in financing curriculum development as being very much in the national interest. It also agreed with the purposes and objectives of the curriculum-study committees, i.e., "to improve teaching and to stimulate the development of more effective teaching materials." The ATPI also recognizes that to attain these objectives, "the curriculum committees must actually prepare, try out and arrange to publish textbooks and collateral or satellite materials for classroom use." But when a government-financed curriculum is copyrighted and its publication is supported by the government, it tends to become monopolizing and to eliminate competition. To avoid the latter, and to allow the curriculum-study committees to make use of the editorial and production expertise of textbook publishers in the preparation of new teaching materials, the ATPI recommends the following course of action for government agencies:

1. Relieve curriculum committees of the responsibility for producing actual classroom teaching and learning materials, and ask them instead to prepare clear and detailed guidelines for the production of such materials.

2. Continue to sponsor summer institutes and teacher training programs, and leave to publishers, and to their authors, the responsibility

for producing in free and open competition the materials needed for use in the classroom.

The ATPI insists that guideline materials must be much more than a scholarly report with recommendations or a blueprint of a course of study with specifications. "[They] must in effect constitute the finest kind of professional program for teachers. Such a set of materials would set clear teaching objectives grade by grade and even unit by unit and give the rationale for these objectives. It should include models of teaching procedures and techniques, even lesson plans, which have been tested and proven by the curriculum committee in school classrooms. It should describe in as much detail as possible the kinds of teaching and learning materials which should be made available if the proposed breakthrough program of the curriculum committee is to be successfully implemented. In some disciplines . . . it will comprise material which will update the reader and give him the subject matter background he needs if he is to understand and appreciate the recommendations of the committee with respect to teaching and learning . . ."

In other words, the ATPI would like to see government-funded curriculum projects produce raw or guideline instructional materials rather than finished ones. They should be placed in the public domain as soon as they have been released to the contracting agency (i.e., OE), to allow publishers and teams of scholars to evaluate their effectiveness, to revise and amend them where necessary, and to test them with teachers, students, parents, and with other educators. This would lead to a "healthy ferment and to a new and searching concern for better teaching in the field in question."

Prototype materials thus released in the public domain would bring an immediate publisher response and "within a surprisingly short time there would not be just one 'authorized' breakthrough set of materials on the market but several competing publications, all produced within the framework established by the recommendations of the curriculum committee."

By placing all instructional materials that are being developed by curriculum-study groups in the public domain, another great deterrent to publisher interest in these programs would be eliminated–i.e., the "baffling detailed publishing problems with which government agencies and curriculum committees are now concerned, especially those relating to rights, terms, contracts, and publisher participation." Unfortunately, royalties derived from federally funded, copyrighted texts go into the general fund of the U.S. Treasury, and not to the sponsoring agency. Therefore, funds are never available for revision of these texts, which usually need updating within four or five years of their publication. Without these royalties no provision can be made for the research necessary for revisions, and the educational community is deprived of the latest developments in the field concerned.

Curtis Benjamin, representing the viewpoint of certain publishers, does not agree with ATPI's position on curriculum-development materials. He objects to a policy that allows the government to place guideline or raw curriculum materials in the public domain for development by commercial publishers, and would prefer that the curriculum-development team continue its work until it has a set of materials ready for classroom use. Once the finished prototype has been released, the sponsoring government agency should arrange for a commercial publisher to publish the report under competitive bidding.

In *Copyright or Public Domain?* Benjamin elucidates his position as follows:

"A successful textbook is usually the product of an ongoing partnership in which the author has continuing professional and proprietary interests. A textbook manuscript is the product not only of the time and effort required to write it but of the author's total professional training and teaching experience as well. His reputation as a scientist and teacher, and often his experience and reputation as an author of other books, are added ingredients. Thus the author's contribution to a successful text is far more than the actual time and effort required to produce a manuscript. Yet under a government contract or grant he is usually paid for that time and effort only. So it is that the author often feels (and rightly, we think) that though the manuscript as a physical property belongs to the government (or to its contracting agency), its style, its methodology, its scholarship, and its authority are still his own. He feels that though the government has clear legal rights in the manuscript, he still has certain professional and proprietary rights in it. Further he usually feels a deep and continuing concern that the integrity of his work shall not be compromised either before or after publication."[23]

Arnold B. Grobman, long-time director of the Biological Sciences Curriculum Study and now at Rutgers University, supports Benjamin's reasoning. Writing in *Science,*[24] he states that "the director of a curriculum project supported by the Office of Education may find it difficult to recruit writers who are seriously interested in producing new curriculum materials for our schools, if they are aware of the possible effects of the public domain policy on their efforts. They would realize that . . . their carefully devised themes and logical presentations could be altered at will by editors and publishers; that they might be completely excluded from the opportunity to revise their original ideas on the basis of actual use in the schools." He counsels against "summarily discarding the traditional rights of an author simply because his work promises to be of public benefit and has therefore been judged worthy of support from public funds."

Benjamin also notes the possibility of distortion, explaining that "once a work has been placed in the public domain, there can be no control whatever over the form or manner in which it is henceforth reproduced and used." For example, "when a work has been placed in the public domain it can be republished under the author's name with additions, deletions, or revisions made by anyone who chooses to do so, provided that the title page carries a notice such as 'Revised by John Doe' or 'With additions by John Doe.' "

He concludes that since government-supported research will result in an increasing number of commercially publishable works, and since the problems of copyright and public interest differ with each publication, a flexible government policy is needed. "Every agency should have a policy under which qualified officers may decide for or against commercial publication of each separate project or program in terms of government benefit and the public interest."

There are occasions, Benjamin agrees, where it is necessary to limit the copyright protection of a government-financed work. He suggests that this be done, however, only after the publisher has had an opportunity to make a reasonable profit on his investment, and the author has had time to realize a reasonable royalty return. Commercial publishers of government-sponsored texts, furthermore, should be allowed to revise them under copyright protection. It has been his experience that two editions of a college text and three editions of a text for elementary or high schools, with a minimal period of ten years in either case, are usually sufficient to perfect and establish a text.

Government support of text revisions has always been an irksome problem. Even government agencies committed to a policy of publication with copyright protection have serious reservations about supporting old curriculum-development projects in this manner. Support of revisions, it is argued, ties up funds that the agencies would rather use for new curriculum projects. Yet publishers have always reserved the right to publish revised editions, a custom that is in direct conflict with a public domain policy. Recognition of this fact is pertinent to any solution of the problem.

The reaction of the community of scholars to the OE public domain policy and the ATPI position brings out another dimension of the problem—one touched upon by Benjamin. The scholars' viewpoint is as follows:

The curriculum developer needs sufficient time to experiment with radical, perhaps even wrong and sloppy ideas. He cannot do this if he is threatened by the possibility of publishers' snatching materials from his desk to disseminate them without his permission or control. He must be guaranteed the opportunity to produce materials that meet his standards of quality. (Scholars like to refer to the drug industry where premature dissemination can do tremendous harm not only to the patients, but also to the developers.) The threat of premature dissemination would seriously inhibit creative thinking as well as the testing of new ideas, and undue emphasis on dissemination, furthermore, may divert his attention from the really significant problems of curriculum development.

Scholars fear that the OE, as a result of its new policy, may be forcing research teams to produce semi-finished materials. This is a questionable practice, for it is not in the public interest to release undemonstrable course curriculums. Consequently, members of the study group may find it necessary to make their own contracts with commercial publishers. There is a great difference in the textbook area between raw and unfinished curriculum materials and those that have been completed, especially as regards the teaching of English, French, Spanish, and other languages. To apply a public domain policy to the intermediate, unfinished stage of a grammar text would be particularly harmful.

There have also been suggestions that OE's public domain policy might cause scholars to be more concerned with their reputation than with their material, and lead them to reserve certain features of their study for inclusion in their own commercially published edition.

It is interesting to note that both publishers and OE officials point to Erwin R. Steinberg's OE-sponsored project[25] at the Carnegie Institute of Technology as the prototype for a guideline, i.e., an unfinished curriculum to be placed in the public domain. Steinberg, however, maintains that his project members did not release to the government an unfinished but rather a completed curriculum, based on a collection of copyrighted English literature. What is different in this instance is the fact that although the lesson plans, etc., are in the public domain, they cannot be used effectively as teaching tools without the copyrighted literature upon which they are based. And since it would cost about $25 to purchase this collection of literature–an outlay few students can afford–a less expensive edition will have to be printed. This can easily be done by a commercial publisher who obtains clearance from the copyright owners for this purpose. In essence, therefore, what the Carnegie Institute team has produced is a completed and tested curriculum. A competing publisher would have no advantage; he could merely arrange for a similar clearance of the copyrighted literature and the teaching plans, tests, questions, etc., would remain the same. Steinberg admits that his is "a peculiar program, oriented in a way which permits a peculiar second stage."

Scholars object to denying members of a curriculum team the right to develop independent contracts with commercial publishers. They consider the thoughts and ideas voiced at annual meetings as being in the public domain, and as being part and parcel of a scholar's contribution to scholarship. But if these ideas or concepts are put into concrete form for use by commercial publishers, then, they feel, consideration should be given to the scholars' proprietary interest therein.

The scholarly community recognizes the validity of the publishers' claim that curriculum evaluation is not yet a precise, scientific art. Disagreeing with certain publishers who maintain that curriculum-development teams orient their research to obtain a "feedback" of their established, a priori, views, and that so-called motivations in curriculum need to be checked and new materials thoroughly scrutinized, scholars do admit that "the evaluation business is a bit dishonest. . . ." As Garlie A. Forehand, chairman of the evaluation section of the Second Carnegie Institute of Technology Conference, says in a draft report:

"Evaluation studies are often built on the model of a psychological experiment. The curriculum defines the independent variable, one level of which is the 'experimental group,' embodying the methods and philosophy of curriculum innovation, and the other, the control or traditionally taught group. This paradigm has been tried and found wanting by a number of evaluators. One difficulty is the impossibility of controlling or isolating the effective features of an experimental curriculum. Another lies in the attempt to define a control group that differs with respect—and only with respect—to the central innovative idea of the experimental curriculum."

Because curriculums are so complex, says Steinberg, "they do not lend themselves as readily to the traditional designs of the psychological experiment as do the psychological experiments from which the designs were drawn. More imaginative approaches to evaluation are obviously necessary. . . ." He offers an illuminating illustration: "When one English teacher tells another, 'when students come out of this course, they know how to read fiction,' the second English teacher thinks that he knows well enough what the speaker means not to have to ask for further definition. The psychologist, however, cannot settle for such a statement. It is not that he does not trust the English teacher, but that he must evaluate in terms of performance. What does 'knowing how to read fiction' mean? If a student 'knows how to read fiction,' what will he do when he reads fiction that a student who does not know how to read fiction will not do? . . . Many English teachers have theories about what the teacher should do to teach the student how to read fiction, but few of them know, in behavioral terms, what they want the student to do as he reads. And yet how are we going to train competent readers unless we do know?"[26]

But, scholars contend, even if the evaluative process of curriculum materials is not yet an exact science, there is still the law of the market place. Teachers, students, and educators are the ones who decide whether a new text is effective and the rule of *caveat emptor* applies.

Scholars claim that the public domain policy of the OE will adversely affect the quality and quantity of scholarly research. Unfortunately, the policy has not been in effect long enough to accumulate significant evidence. In the short time it has been operating, university directors of research have found that the quantity of research has not been affected. University scholars applying for government grants have accepted the OE ruling without demurral. With the exception of curriculum studies, the university scholar is principally interested in being able to publish his report in a scholarly journal, or as a monograph—even without royalty. He also wishes to be free to discuss it. Some directors have indicated that even when the grant or contract allows for copyright, scholars have often failed to take advantage of this privilege. By the same token, there are some university research offices, notably at Harvard, that are not interested in promoting and negotiating contracts for profit with publishers. Even if the OE would waive its public domain policy, Harvard would not take advantage of it.

Supporting the contention that the quantity of research has not been affected by the OE policy is the growing number of scholars who apply for government grants to finance research. It should be noted, however, that the amount of money appropriated by Congress for OE research has increased appreciably, and this factor alone could account for the increasing number of applications. Then again, university research directors caution that, when the effect of the public domain policy is fully realized by the academic community, it will not be as complaisant about it—especially with reference to release of curriculum materials at interim stages. Some university scholars have already taken a strong position on the premature release of curriculum materials and have declared that they would, unequivocally, refuse to contract for any curriculum-development project that requires public domain to take effect before the final product has been released by the developing team.

It is not too clear, either, how the public domain policy has affected the quality of the work produced. It has been suggested, for example, that the quality of a project released at an interim stage could be somewhat deceiving. Other scholars, for instance, impressed by the seeming excellence of the materials, could use them and be unaware of the possibility for failure inherent in this stage of development. This could have deleterious results and reflect badly on the developing team. It is also within the realm of possibility that the OE public domain policy would influence the developing team not to release certain controversial or experimental and unproven features of its work at the interim stage.

There is one other aspect that deserves to be mentioned in this context. According to Louis Ferman, director of industrial research at the University of Michigan, it is a rare occasion when a well-written, completed report is handed to the government agency at the end of a project. Usually government grants terminate while the research is still going on or as it is just about to end. The final report then has to be written on the scholar's or study team's own time, a situation that is not conducive to turning out a highly polished product.

One of the main difficulties in arriving upon a judgment of OE's public domain policy is that it is entirely too new to test its validity. It still remains to be seen whether it is the best way in which the government can meet the diverse public interests involved.

The use of public funds is a key factor in the public domain controversy. Government funds to support research in education are invested not only to improve the quality of education but to make reports of this research widely available, in the shortest time and with a minimum of restrictions. As government-sponsored research is intended to stimulate additional research and increased use of the new findings, dissemination and accessibility to the public are also important. And if the government wants the private sector to disseminate these federally sponsored research reports, ways will have to be found to protect that sector's investment, bearing the public interest in mind.

It is suggested that the OE use public funds for the following purposes:

1. To attract the best scholarship both in government and in the private sector.
2. To arrange for the best dissemination of the information and conceptual principles arrived at by this scholarly community.
3. To assure the public's right of accessibility to information.
4. To assure that their use benefits a broad segment of the public.
5. To assure that there be no unjust enrichment of the private sector at the expense of the public sector.
6. To assure that they are used in such a manner as not to give competitive advantage to a few.
7. To encourage cooperation between the public and the private sectors in the development of curriculum materials (both in the funding of the work and in the pooling of ideas and resources).

Public Domain Policy: Conclusions and Recommendations

> "Technological advances can make their greatest contribution to educational improvements if we have a close give-and-take between the 'hardware' and the 'software' people, so that they share understandings and objectives. . . . *The key word is more than cooperation; it is creative cooperation.* We look to industry not only to fulfill our demands and prescriptions but, in the characteristic manner of American industry, to provide innovative and original contributions to the educational process itself. *We will have to share problems, tell you of our needs, our pressures, our successes and our failures. We hope you will do the same.* In the past, there has not been enough of this teamwork. The solutions lie not only in engineering, but in an understanding of the people of the United States–their tolerances, their goals, and their aspirations for their children and their society."[27] (Italics added)

This eloquent appeal by the Commissioner of Education, Harold Howe II, suggests the frame of reference in which a public domain policy may reasonably be considered, i.e., "creative cooperation." For both the government and the private sector obviously have mutual interests in the production and dissemination of scientific and technical research reports, and the national welfare can be greatly improved by this cooperation.

But, before creative cooperation can be achieved, a balance must be struck between the interest of the private sector in its own viability and the interest of the public in the preservation of its democratic institutions. In essence, the basic question is how to keep knowledge and the economy free. With so many diverse and partisan interests involved, it would appear that the answer lies not in a single, inflexible government policy on public domain, but rather in a recognition of more than one policy. What is needed is a coordination of several policies, reflecting deliberate choices made from carefully evaluated alternatives, whose aim it would be, as Commissioner Howe states, not merely to achieve cooperation, but creative cooperation, between the private sector and the government.

In arriving at a coordination of several policies, consideration must be given to certain premises.

1. Not only is the federal government playing and will continue to play a dominant role in research and development in the United States, but the private sector concedes that it depends on the government to finance the great bulk of its research activity. The federal government is in a more favorable position than the private sector to invest in research, because it is not obligated to make a profit. Even the largest commercial publishers are unable to spend unlimited funds on research projects. The government, on the other hand, has the obligation to use public funds for the public interest and must therefore follow an aggressive program of research and dissemination even in doubtful areas. The government, furthermore, does not depend entirely on its own resources, nor does it pay the entire cost of research. Scholars, educa-

tors, non-profit institutions and even the private sector make a considerable contribution to the research and development efforts of the government. The government can also afford a greater degree of economic waste than the private sector.

2. The information explosion and the government's involvement in research development are changing the traditional patterns that have existed in these areas. Today, for example, research for curriculum development is basically work done "for hire" by scholars and others, for institutions of higher learning or related associations, on compensated released time. In the past, textbooks were written independently by educators and other interested persons, on their own time, and their sale to commercial publishers was negotiated privately. Present-day knowledge has outgrown the individual research entrepreneur. Instead, teams of specialists in different disciplines work together and prepare the materials for a new curriculum. The entire approach to the features of control, financing, royalties, and honoraria, therefore, must be changed, and an effort must be made to arrange for equitable returns to all concerned. The question of how federal research funds can be kept flowing to the scholarly and research community without imposing inhibiting controls will eventually have to be answered.

3. It is still possible for scholars and researchers, working independently with some financial help from a government agency such as the OE, to produce a report on a subject investigated and commented on in a manageable area of knowledge. The distinction between the publication and dissemination of these research reports and of the government-supported research produced by large-scale team efforts, such as in the curriculum area, should be recognized.

4. Through its Government Printing Office and its information centers, the government is able to print and distribute research reports produced with public funds. There is general agreement, however, that

commercial publishers at present can publish and disseminate these reports better than the government and, by reason of their editorial resources, can also produce a better report.

5. The government lacks the organization and administrative personnel to publish and distribute curriculum materials developed with public funds by curriculum-study centers and similar institutions. The study centers themselves are even less well equipped to do so. An equitable solution with reference to publication rights therefore must reflect the objectives of the government in supporting such research, the interests of the taxpayers, of the members of the research teams, and of the commercial publishers.

6. If it is not in the public interest for the government to publish a publicly supported research report or curriculum, the private sector should be encouraged to do so on an equitable basis.

7. In trying to arrive at an equitable solution to the problem of the publishers' rights versus the public's interest in government-supported research, major consideration must be given to society's educational needs and how best to meet them.

8. To avoid undue government influence in the development of publicly supported curriculum materials, scholars engaged in these projects must be free to exercise their professional judgment as to the scope and content of these materials.

9. It is in the public interest for government-financed curriculum materials to achieve recognition in the competitive educational market, without promotional support by the sponsoring agency. This will leave the traditional responsibility of determining what should be taught in the schools to the appropriate local school authorities. As these materials will be neither owned nor endorsed by the sponsoring government agency, the private sector must be encouraged to contribute through packaging, introducing and disseminating them in the educational mar-

ket. Because of this interdependent relationship, rights in these materials must reflect the public interest as well as the interest of the private sector.

10. The public's stake in the proper dissemination of and accessibility to government-developed research reports, studies, and information must be preserved. Reservation of the government's rights to use these materials, even if commercially published, on an irrevocable, royalty-free, non-exclusive license basis must be accepted.

11. Participation of university scholars and educators in elementary and high school curriculum-development materials should be encouraged. The greatest problems, as well as the greatest opportunity for profit, lie in the "el-hi" textbook field. The situation is different in the college textbook field.

12. The rule of the educational market place governs the acceptance of new curriculum materials. It is questionable whether guideline prototype curriculum materials can be developed sufficiently to meet the criteria established by the ATPI—some educators seriously doubt it. A policy decision on the issue of guideline prototypes versus finished prototypes should reflect the realization that the ultimate benefit applies to the same educational community, i.e., the same publishers, the same authors, the same public.

13. The diversity of rulings by the various federal agencies on public domain policy and publishing contracts for government-supported research products is objectionable. Uniformity in this area is most desirable since inconsistency creates unnecessary difficulties. Recognition, however, should be given to national security interests. An enabling law or an executive regulation should prescribe a general policy for all federal agencies to avoid having one agency use one policy and another agency a different one for the same situation.

In conclusion, therefore, the following course with reference to government-supported research and the public domain is suggested:

To meet the objectives of the Office of Education to produce instructional materials of the highest quality with federal funds; to ensure use and study of these materials by widely disseminating them; to meet the desire of scholars for recognition of authorship, of integrity of their work, and for some assurance of financial rewards; to encourage the participation of commercial publishers in the packaging, production, introduction, and dissemination of these educational materials; to make improved curriculum materials readily available; to ensure that public funds will not be used to give competitive advantage or unjust enrichment to a few, and that society's resources be focused on the improvement of education–it would appear that OE's all-encompassing public domain policy must be replaced by one that recognizes certain proprietary rights at one stage of research and provides for a public domain policy at another.

Certainly, it cannot be said that the OE public domain policy has ensured the production of instructional materials of the highest quality. Nor does it appear that the OE policy guarantees the widest dissemination of such materials, especially in view of the private sector's reluctance to participate in the program without preservation of its traditional and customary rights. This is especially significant in an area where the government and the prime contractors (universities and study centers) lack the interest and organization to publish, disseminate, and promote improved curriculum materials produced with federal funds. While it has not been definitively demonstrated that the OE public domain policy has had an adverse effect on the quantity and quality of curriculum-development work, neither has it been demonstrated that this policy has met OE's objectives in establishing it initially.

As long as the Office of Education is willing to support scholars and educators with grants and contracts for curriculum development, it should respect the developing team's objectives. It is suggested, therefore, that the OE acknowledge that curriculum materials developed under grants or contracts be considered either as "raw," or "guideline," or "preliminary," or "unfinished," or essentially "finished," or "complete" prototypes or models, depending upon the development team's judgment as to which version best meets their objectives and purposes. This question should be determined by the developing teams rather than OE officials or publishers' representatives, for the teams know best what is in the interest of a program's integrity and premise. To insist that curriculum-development teams be limited to producing guideline prototypes, despite their opposition to such a policy, and that intermediate reports of untried and untested material be placed in the public domain immediately upon release by the team even against its better judgment, is not sensible. It may be preferable, therefore, to develop a modified plan that provides for some curriculum materials to be placed in the public domain, especially those concerned with courses, while others be granted a period of experimentation.

Curriculum-development teams, through their contracting agency (university or other non-profit organization), should be given exclusive control (copyright) over all curriculum materials that they produce, including texts, manuals, films, apparatus, tests, specifications, etc., for the period of the OE grant or contract. During this period the materials should be made available for widespread dissemination in a preliminary or experimental form to all persons, institutions, or government agencies having a reasonable and legitimate interest in them. The cost of this distribution should be borne by the government under the terms of the contract or grant.

In consideration of this exclusive control over the materials, the members of the curriculum-development team will agree not to use or authorize the use of any part of these materials in commercial publication form. This will allow for a period of creative privacy in which the team will be assured the opportunity to offer for public use, as indicated above, to all persons, institutions or government agencies having an interest in these materials, products that it believes represent its best professional efforts.

Upon conclusion of the project, team members will distribute what may be the final form of their materials to participating schools and other interested parties, royalty-free and without compensation to themselves or to the curriculum-development project. Inasmuch as the team's exclusive control during this period serves only to preserve the integrity of their work, it will not give them such a proprietary interest in the materials as to prevent others from critically analyzing and evaluating the work for subsequent independent revision or modification. Commercial publishers, for instance, would have an opportunity to consider a team's curriculum materials for the purpose of publishing them in different versions, working either with other, competing teams or even with the members of the original team.

Upon the termination of the grant or contract term, the materials will go into the public domain. However, for a moratorium period of one year no one, not even the members of the team, can publish the materials thus released. This moratorium period will afford publishers as well as team members, interested in developing commercial editions of the materials, an equal opportunity to do so. It will give the publishers, furthermore, a chance to examine the final materials and decide how to proceed, either in cooperation with the original team members or with competing teams.

By letting the team members have control over the interim materials, the government safeguards the integrity of their work and allows them to produce raw or finished materials, as they desire. When the government agency releases these materials in the public domain, it could—to protect the team's authorship—require that publishers who want to develop their own versions acknowledge the project, authors, and the original source of support. Of course, any part of the interim materials that had been otherwise copyrighted would be subject to the fair-use doctrine.

To protect the interests of the government, the agency involved would also obtain from the copyright holders a royalty-free license to use as it wants all materials produced with federal funds and to produce and disseminate them for its own purposes.

The position of the ATPI is that all curriculum-development materials should be placed in the public domain as soon as released, even if they are still in an experimental stage. The ATPI also insists that guideline or raw prototype materials instead of finished materials be developed. In view of the fact, however, that the success or failure of the new materials will be determined on the educational market place, it is submitted that the publishers have little to lose by letting the scholars develop their materials as they deem necessary. By placing the final report in the public domain, the federal agency is relieved of the burden of administrative control over its publication. It is also relieved of the added difficulty of having to decide whether to support a revision five or six years later. And as long as the agency refrains from promoting a copyrighted version of a report, a recurrence of the PSSC textbook incident is unlikely. Publishers on their part will have to invest money to publish, package, and promote curriculum materials in the educational market. Since the market is highly competitive, the materials will have to be properly priced, so that the public interest is protected in that respect, too.

Another fear the ATPI has is that the development of completed prototype materials will lead to a national curriculum. It is submitted that this will not occur if the government agency releases these materials in the public domain without promoting them. They will be prototypes, to be sure, but the 30,000 or so school districts that dominate the "el-hi" educational system guarantee a considerable diversity, which private enterprise supports through its competitive system.

Since the U.S. government plays a primary role in scientific and technical research and development, most of the worth-while publications ensuing from such research and development are potentially within the government's sphere of control.

The American Textbook Publishers Institute takes the position that scholarly, scientific, and technical research reports are unique. It maintains that there can be only one definitive edition of Melville, only one General Theory of Relativity, and that for works of this unique character the national goal must be the widest possible circulation at the lowest cost and greatest speed. The marketing techniques of commercial publishers, the ATPI maintains, afford the optimum means of achieving this goal. Their investment, however, in typesetting, platemaking, art work, promotion, and distribution should be protected by exclusive rights for the time required to recapture these costs. It is in the public interest, therefore, according to the ATPI, for federal agencies to permit contractors to copyright government-financed, scholarly, scientific and technical works for at least ten years, following which they would become public domain property.

It should be recognized, however, that not all government-funded research results in valuable publishing property. There is no doubt that many reports are merely "run of the mill" documents, poorly prepared and greatly in need of editing. This is an area where the commercial publisher can play a valuable role. No publisher, however, will want to invest time and capital in these reports, if he has no copyright protection. Failure to grant this copyright protection may have the effect of narrowing rather than broadening the dissemination of a report.

Publishers, furthermore, insist that the public domain policy is needlessly absolute and restrictive and has an adverse effect on governmental, public, and publishing interests. They advocate a flexible policy where federally funded scholarly, technical, and scientific works are concerned and can see no legal reason why a non-government independent contractor or grantee should not secure copyright in works prepared by him under a government contract or grant, as long as the contract or grant provides for it.

The Office of Education's position on scientific and technical research reports is that a public domain policy for these works will improve the quality of research, and that research produced with public funds should become public property. This latter viewpoint is represented also by Senator Long who objects to copyrighting federally funded research reports because public investment should not be permitted to result in private franchise or privilege, and information prepared at government expense should be freely available to the public.

Once again, it is submitted that the solution to the problem does not lie in an inflexible public domain policy but rather in a flexible one that also recognizes the technological developments that are taking place in the information storage and retrieval field. Actually, these developments are so dynamic that the question of whether the research reports are served best by a public domain policy or by a copyright policy may soon be immaterial.

The fact that technical and scientific publishing may in the near future be replaced by information storage and retrieval systems was brought out by no less an august group than the President's Science Advisory Committee. In its report dated January 10, 1963, entitled *Science, Government, and Information,* the committee noted:

"The growth of published information has fostered the invention of many new handling and searching techniques and concepts. Best known are the retrieval systems based on automatic machinery. In addition, there are imaginative new ways of listing titles (for example, permuted titles), of gaining access to the literature (citation indexes), of preparing abstracts or translations (by machine), of compacting the physical size of the record (microfilm and microfiches), of duplicating printed material.

"The invention of the new retrieval methods is beginning to affect our traditional modes of communication. The traditional forms of the book, journal, and reprint may eventually give way to the machine storage of graphical and digital information and machine-generated copy. The technical publishing business may gradually be transformed into the information handling business in which the printing press as a means of mass production of identical documents no longer plays a dominant role."[28]

The government's awareness of the revolutionary implications of the information explosion and the new technology, and the profound challenge these offer not only to information control and retrieval but also to document production, reproduction, and transfer, is shown by the fact that in 1964 alone it supported some 200 scientific and technical information studies.[29]

Characteristic of the capabilities of these new systems is the description of a proposed library for the Rome Air Development Center of the U.S. Air Force, recommended more than three years ago by an American Library Association Study Group:

"Using xerographic printers, report duplicates in hard copy could be prepared locally. Or, with facsimile, it would be possible to scan the basic report in the center and have it reproduced miles away at a remote regional location. It could also be scanned with video and reviewed on a TV monitor elsewhere. Finally, it could be duplicated on file in its microform and forwarded to the user that way. In any event, the integrity of the basic file would remain intact and the electronic center would become a duplicating rather than a circulating library."[30]

The alarming aspect of the knowledge explosion was touched upon by Vannevar Bush, who warned that with approximately 60 million pages of scientific and technical information published annually, science may well become "bogged down in its own products." Two factors compound the problem: the amount of information available on a specific subject is steadily increasing, and so is the rate of obsolescence of this information. As reported in the New York *Times,*[31] Seymour H. Farber of the University of California Medical School predicted that the major portion of some 145,000 bibliographical entries in the 1964 *Index Medicus* would be obsolete in five years. The new technology, therefore, must be used not only to store and retrieve documents, but also to retrieve information and remove obsolete material. Unless most of the scientific and technical materials now available can be taken advantage of quickly, they may be wasted. The prime need of the public and the private sector thus is immediate accessibility to all the knowledge that research and development have uncovered.

This need and the emerging technological developments have contributed to the evolving of new information-retrieval patterns in government agencies. Federally financed information centers are beginning to replace conventional information media such as scientific and technical reports and journals. Instead of issuing their scientific and technical reports in the traditional way, some of the major agencies–notably NASA, the AEC, the Clearinghouse for Federal Science and Technical Information, the Defense Documentation Center of the Office of Education – are disseminating some of them on microfiches. Due to the agencies' growing involvement in the dissemination of research reports and the government's plans for a national information-retrieval network, it is likely that federally funded materials will increasingly be disseminated through information centers–either in microfilm or hard copy or by remote transmission.

Lowell Hattery offers some interesting statistics and points to the operations of the Clearinghouse for Federal Science and Technical Information as a case in point. Established in 1964 as an agency of the Department of Commerce to replace the Office of Technical Services, it collects and disseminates scientific, technical and engineering information. It sells reports of federally supported research and also serves as a sales agent for the Superintendent of Documents. Reports are sold either in the form of the usual, printed hard copy or as a microfiche, with the price based on the cost of reproduction and handling. According to Hattery, the Clearinghouse during the first four months of fiscal 1966 shipped more than 600,000 copies of documents of which more than a third went–free of charge–to Department of Defense contractors and others served by the Defense Documentation Center. During the same four-month period more than 20,000 microfiche duplicates were prepared. The document collection of the Clearinghouse at present consists of about 450,000 titles with a current annual increase of about 75,000 documents.

NASA's microfiche program is indicative of the new document-handling role of the government. Its purpose is to provide NASA researchers and other interested personnel with technical information by offering bibliographical control of the world's literature on aerospace research findings, and by announcing and disseminating this literature in the shortest possible time. NASA has awarded Documentation, Inc., in Bethesda, Md., a contract to index, analyze and abstract all the literature and to reproduce it on microfiches. Journals of abstracts then call the material to the attention of interested scholars, *et al.* Approximately 50,000 titles are thus processed annually. Hattery found that microfiche production and distribution to NASA research centers, contractors, universities and other organizations amounted to 3,500,000 in 1964, to five million in 1965, and is estimated to reach seven million in 1966.

NASA believes it can soon reduce the charge for a microfiche from 10 cents to less than 1 cent. A new project now in development, known as MARIAN, will permit researchers to query NASA's information store without having to go through a programer. The MARIAN prototype, according to its technical director, "will probably be a network linking NASA headquarters with one or two research centers. An operational system could serve not only other NASA centers but major research and development contractors as well."

In view of the foregoing, there is hardly any doubt that the federal government's sale of research reports through mechanized storage and information systems will not only have a marked impact on traditional technical and scientific publishing, but will also place the public domain question in a different perspective.

COSATI, an acronym for the Committee on Scientific and Technical Information, represents an even more dramatic development in the information storage and retrieval field. According to William T. Knox, its chairman, it is charged with improving the performance of current and near-future federal agency programs in the scientific and engineering disciplines, and with coordinating them. COSATI, for example, is concerned with "acquisition, accession, abstracting, indexing, announcement, distribution, terminology control, equipment compatibility and convertibility, wholesale and retail sources, specialized information centers, libraries, and depositories." It is also involved in making recommendations for the orderly development of information-science technology. As a result of a report it received in 1965 from the System Development Corporation, COSATI is now considering the feasibility of making available in the U.S. at least one copy of every publication of worldwide scientific and technical significance. It is also recommending an integrated national network of information and document retrieval systems in the fields of science and technology.

Thus not only is the government involved in scientific communication, but its involvement is growing rapidly. Federal agencies are discovering that the "non-book" approach allows them more freedom and control over information and knowledge developed under government grant or contract than the traditional book approach. Reliance on the GPO to produce and disseminate their research reports is gradually disappearing, and except for special publishing situations, the agencies' interest in the commercial publication of their funded reports is also waning. National information services will naturally incorporate these reports, as well as substitutes, derivations, and hard copies. The time is as close as 1975 when, according to Knox, a national, fully responsive, remote interrogation system with tape files will be available.

The Office of Education is similarly developing its own information network, which has come to be known as ERIC (Educational Research Information Center). It is a decentralized, nationwide network of information clearinghouses and research documentation centers, coordinated with the Office of Education. In order to provide the public with reliable current educational research and related information promptly and inexpensively, ERIC will acquire, abstract, index, store, retrieve, and disseminate educational research documents throughout the nation. All OE research publications from 1954 to date will eventually be stored and serviced by ERIC. Satellite centers will select and store the documents based on the subject specialty of each center. One document in every five examined so far has been found acceptable; it is estimated that the ERIC system will grow by 10,000 documents a year.[32] ERIC periodically announces the availability of documents in bulletin listings, and will on request supply bibliographies and abstracts; it will also provide reproductions either in hard copy at 4 cents a page or in microfiche form at 9 cents a fiche. (A four-by-six-inch fiche holds between sixty and seventy pages, at an 18:1 reduction.) According to Lee G. Burchinal and Harold A. Haswell of the OE, "the day is not far distant when the ERIC network will link universities, professional organizations, school systems, boards of education–the entire educational community–to speed all research results to places where they are needed and when they are needed." Since August 1965, under P.L. 89-10 programs, ERIC has distributed more than 15 million pages of information in microfiche form. At present ERIC seeks permission from copyright holders to copy from their work, and orders for material are generally filled within five days of being requested. ERIC's document-reproduction service is operated under an OE contract by Bell & Howell's Micro Photo Division. The OE also uses the clearinghouse to notify scholars and researchers in education of the availability of its reports.

Lee Deighton, of Macmillan, recently analyzed the importance of these developments for the future. "Rather soon," he believes, "it will be government policy that all products of federally funded research must go into the information networks established by the government." Although he admits that "the potential gain to our society will be very great," and that "we cannot reasonably complain about the loss to private printing and publishing of scientific and technical data and reports emerging from government-funded research if this information is presented more suitably in microform than in journals or books," he maintains that the federal government is no match for the private sector in the distribution of printed materials. "The interests of public information can be served only by private commercial publication under the protection of the Constitution." He doubts that free men can ever "willingly turn over to government the full control of information in any area." Commercial publishing and printing will suffer great losses, though, he predicts, if the government information system is developed to the point where it will contain all significant information – from whatever source and in whatever form.

As government agencies increasingly place their reports of federally supported technical and scientific research into document-storage and information-retrieval systems, it would appear that the public domain policy of the Office of Education will hinder rather than promote creative cooperation between the government and the private sector, and that the OE could achieve the objective it is seeking by spending public funds in research without an unequivocal public domain policy. It may be preferable, therefore, for the OE as well as the other grant agencies to consider a more flexible, discretionary program, which would emerge if they were to incorporate some of the recommendations listed below.

The sweeping policy of public domain for government-sponsored research reports should be abandoned whenever the public interest demands it. Instead, the agencies should accept the principle expressed in section 105 of the proposed copyright law revision, which continues the present prohibition against copyright in published works of the government, but recognizes that this does not arbitrarily apply to commercial publications resulting from government support of research. To repeat the words of the Register of Copyrights, "There should be nothing to prohibit an independent contractor or grantee from securing copyright in works prepared by him under a government contract or grant, as long as the contract or grant permits it."

At present many government agencies have complete discretion in the type of grants and contracts they negotiate for the publication of research results. They can insist on a royalty payment to the government or refrain from it in order to keep the price down; they can place the materials in the public domain or not, according to the needs of the situation. This policy would fit in well with the government's information-retrieval objectives and would also permit the private sector to make its contribution to the production and dissemination of these reports. The provision that allows such discretionary powers is part of many government contracts or research grants and has generally been accepted by the private sector. In essence, it permits copyrighted commercial publication under the following condition:

> When in contracts for research the contracting officer determines, in accordance with department procedures, that public dissemination of the work, or certain designated parts of the work specified to be delivered under contract, is in the best interest of the government and would be facilitated by the government relinquishing its rights to publish for sale or to have others publish for sale for it. . . .

Instead of providing in the contract, however, that it agrees to refrain from publishing such work for sale or from authorizing others to do so if the contracting party publishes the report, the government should include the following clause:

> Any such copyrighted publication shall be subject to a royalty-free, non-exclusive, and irrevocable license to the government to reproduce [the materials], translate them, publish them, use and dispose of them and to authorize others to do so.

In a sense, these clauses would permit a continuation of the old status quo and yet would also be applicable to the new information services the government is developing. The present OE public domain policy appears to prohibit private exploitation of public research projects, instead of being sufficiently flexible to allow the operation of both, copyright protection and public domain. Creators of government-sponsored research reports should be permitted to negotiate privately with publishers to promote and even exploit the substance of their reports when it is in the public interest, for instance, when it is evident that the GPO cannot do as good an editorial, publishing, promotion, and dissemination job as the commercial publisher, or when the situation requires controlled dissemination, such as in the case of psychological personality-assessment devices where there is need to avoid invasion of privacy. If the agency desires to limit profits, it could arrange for part of the royalties to be returned, or it could ask for an assignment of copyright to the government and a license in return for exclusive publication rights for a limited period of time.

There is no reason to believe that the commercial publishers will publish government-supported research reports without copyright protection unless these reports are so popular that more than one publisher can make a profit in competition with others and the GPO.

Actually, the government has nothing to lose by providing copyright protection for those reports that for the public interest's sake merit commercial publication. Many of them will in the foreseeable future be placed directly on microfiches; by reason of the royalty-free, nonexclusive, and irrevocable license it obtains, the government will be free to use them for its document-storage and information-retrieval systems. Hence, they would be publicly accessible despite the copyright protection. Commercial publishers will also gain by this arrangement, for they will be given the opportunity to publish selected federally supported research reports with copyright protection. In addition, they will be in a position to recover estimated losses ensuing from the government's reservation of the right to reproduce and sell these works, by negotiating more advantageous royalty terms with the initiating agency at the contract stage. Such an arrangement would allow for public and commercial publication with a combination of copyright protection and public domain policy, depending on what the public interest demands. It appears that there is a market for both the byproducts of

ERIC and the copyrighted commercial publications of OE materials. A sufficient number of researchers would probably prefer to buy commercially published reports instead of ERIC microfiches or print-outs—provided they are priced competitively to make commercial publications economically feasible.

In arranging for the publication of copyrighted editions of government-sponsored reports, the government could allow the grantee or contracting party to negotiate his own terms with the publisher, subject to supervision by the granting agency, or the agency itself could arrange the contracting terms. Some agencies object to the administration of these contracts as particularly burdensome. Publishers for their part object to the different rules of the various agencies and would prefer uniform regulations that would be enforced by all agencies. Something like this could be accomplished if, for instance, all agencies adhered to a policy of closed competitive bidding, considering the lowest price to the buyer, a number of copies given free to the government, royalty payments to the government and/or the author, paper, design, etc.

The government should also consider the possibility of establishing a common policy on publicly supported research reports and having it centrally administered. This could be done, for instance, through a presidential or standing committee, such as a joint House-Senate committee, which would work closely with the Bureau of the Budget.

Accessibility of Information

Related to the public domain problems is the equally important issue of access to information. There are many obstacles to the availability and use of information developed by government-financed research and development. A substantial portion of this information is simply never disclosed or only to limited sources. Richard Barber notes that, although the government now supports well over two-thirds of the country's scientific effort, it directly accounts for the expenditure of only one dollar in five. "Most of the work is actually done outside the government, primarily by large industrial corporations. Of all the information generated in this connection, little is ever accessible beyond the tightly restricted confines of both government agencies and contractors."[33]

M. B. Schnapper asserts that dissemination of publicly financed research through official publication by government agencies is almost inconsequential. Only a negligible portion of such publication is in truth accessible to the public. Schnapper has determined that only 2½ percent of the $274 million spent by the government in 1965 for printing was allocated for copies of publications available to the public through the Superintendent of Documents. The reasons for this limited policy are that 1) much government printing is of extralegal security ("restricted" or "official use only"), and 2) many agencies simply neglect to make their publications available through the Superintendent of Documents. Barber adds that there are very few laws that require government agencies to make their publications available to the public. In fact, a sponsoring agency has to authorize the Superintendent of Documents to sell its publications, and exercises considerable discretion over their dissemination through its own channels. It is Barber's belief also "that the results of government-financed research should be freely available to the public and not encumbered by the monopolistic restrictions afforded by copyright."

Since maximum accessibility to information prepared at government expense is becoming increasingly important, each agency should know what materials are available in other agencies, including "security" or "tentative draft" material. Determination as to availability of the material and the supervision of indexing could be handled by a central board within the federal government, consisting of representatives of all Cabinet departments and certain key agencies, but with the decision-making powers in the hands of a few recognized and experienced men.

The board would have to establish rules and regulations with reference to the following: 1) Bureaucratic competition. 2) Needs and merits of secrecy. 3) Necessity of indexing to avoid duplication of research. 4) Identification of ongoing research projects so that formal titles will not cause misleading or incomplete indexing. 5) Indexing of the research work that is being done by non-government employees and is of value to the government.

Another complex issue, closely related to that of security, is the problem of defining a study and its completion. Agencies wishing to keep information private as long as possible may combine several studies into one large project and contend that this project should not be released until all studies are completed. Completion, furthermore, is an uncertain term, because some agencies encourage their grantees and consultants to let agency officials look at "working papers," and not to submit a completed report. There appears to be no way to eliminate these difficulties entirely. However, some means should be found within the civil service system and/or the jurisdiction of presidential assistants to discourage such tactics. Of course, the requirement to index studies once they have begun should provide a fairly effective method of checking on the completion and agency definition of a study.

Consideration will also have to be given to restrictions on the use or misuse of materials—when, for instance, may tentative conclusions be treated as determinative? Clear labeling of studies and/or conclusions as tentative will help avoid difficulties. In general, the benefits of availability, including an increased possibility for constructive criticism, outweigh the dangers of misuse of tentative conclusions. The chance of having these conclusions misinterpreted is a major deterrent to making only the summaries of studies available (which may not be correct or may not reveal deficiencies in the study technique). Another problem is the use of studies by those not qualified to do so, for instance, professionally unqualified laymen who request access to materials involving the administration of psychological tests.

Protection of the right of privacy and confidential disclosure may be another reason to restrict the use of certain government studies by the general public. This can occur when participation in a study is conditioned on the promise not to reveal the participant's name or to reveal it only to a limited group (e.g., the AEC). It could also happen when a study uses materials furnished by the government for purposes unrelated to the study (e.g., use of Internal Revenue Service returns in the study of corporate structure, where even if names are omitted, it is still possible to identify corporations and/or their officers). These are instances when it would be preferable to make nothing but abstracts available to the public.

Accessibility to government-sponsored research reports will be increased once all public materials deemed accessible to the public have been processed for inclusion in the document-storage and information-retrieval systems that the government is developing. The granting of copyright to commercial publishers would make the materials accessible to those who wanted them in hard-cover form, and those who prefer microfiches could obtain them from the government.

Reprography and Intellectual Property

Speaking to the 1966 Congress of Poets, Playwrights, Editors, Essayists and Novelists (P.E.N.), Marshall McLuhan noted with characteristic insight: "In the age of Xerox, the reader becomes a publisher and so does the schoolroom." In essence, this is exactly what commercial publishers fear. Photocopying of the printed page is becoming so easy and inexpensive, they lament, that if it is allowed to continue without control they will be forced out of business. Publishers view the current photocopying production, estimated to be in the vicinity of 12 billion copies annually, with alarm, and despair over the statement by C. Peter McColough, executive vice president of Xerox, that "by 1969, some 25 billion impressions will be made by copiers, and the information explosion will still be accelerating."

Scholars have always felt free to copy by hand the works of others for their own research and study needs. When copying machines became readily available, it was a simple transition for the scholar to extend his note-taking to photocopying from copyrighted material. Publishers had accepted copying by hand because they were aware of the physical limitations involved in such a process. With the advent of the machine copier, however, the situation has radically changed, and the publishers have begun to object to the scholars' photocopying copyrighted scientific and technical materials without compensation to the copyright holder. If photocopying is allowed to increase, what will happen to the copyright owner's market for his work? The publishers are afraid that it will become so small that they will have to cease publishing. Eventually, they claim, there will be nothing left for the scholars to photocopy.

The educators have taken issue with the publishers in this area. They maintain that they have no economic motivation in making multiple photocopies of copyrighted materials for classroom use, that they are not doing it for a profit, nor for any direct or indirect commercial advantage.

The publishers agree but point out that they are being deprived of profit. "We will lose sales through your use of photocopies," they say, and add that as far as textbooks and other instructional materials are concerned, "the sole market is the schools, which usually buy multiple copies." If school systems are permitted to make copies, "the market for published books is destroyed."

The struggle between the commercial publishers and the educators over this right to photocopy concerns principally the proposed revision of the copyright law. The Register of Copyrights has contended that the revised bill "would in no way whatsoever diminish the privilege that schools now have under the present law with respect to classroom uses of copyrighted materials. Anything that can be done under the doctrine of fair use now could be done under the bill, and the bill, even more clearly than the present law, completely exempts performances and exhibitions in classrooms and in-school instructional broadcasts. . . . While the present law contains a 'for profit' limitation with respect to the right of public performance, the right of copying is an absolute right, unqualified by any 'for profit' limitation. Any non-profit copying under the present law could clearly constitute infringement unless the doctrine of fair use were applicable."[34]

Despite the objections of the educators to this view, it appears that the doctrine of fair use is the device that will eventually control the *legal* aspects of photocopying for classroom use.

Librarians have also taken a position on photocopying. The 1964 findings of the Joint Libraries Committee on Fair Use in Photocopying are as follows:

1. The making of a single copy by a library is a direct and natural extension of traditional library service.
2. Such service, employing modern copying methods, has become essential.
3. The present demand can be satisfied without inflicting measurable damage on publishers and copyright owners.
4. Improved copying processes will not materially affect the demand for single-copy library duplication for research purposes.

Librarians and educators, aside from the merits of their arguments in favor of photocopying, are honestly concerned about their rights under the doctrine of fair use. The fair-use concept is an elusive one and for the layman quite difficult to implement. Fair use is an exception to the rule that copies may not be made of copyrighted materials without permission of the copyright owner. The courts still apply the guidelines laid down by Mr. Justice Story in 1841[35] to determine whether a violation of fair use has occurred. "We must . . . in deciding questions of this sort, look to the nature and objects of the selections made, the quantity and value of the materials used, and the degree in which the use may prejudice the sale, or diminish the profits, or supersede the objects of the original work." Although the educators say they have difficulty adhering to these guidelines, the publishers emphasize that no teacher has ever been sued for infringement of copyright because of classroom use. But how does this concept fit into the development of educational television and community antenna television (CATV) which relays entire educational programs to subscribers? Actually, educational television is easier to control with reference to copyright infringement than photocopying, since ETV is not a simple and private act as is photocopying.

Publishers further maintain that "the predominant use of copyrighted materials in schools is the use of excerpts. Encyclopedias, dictionaries, handbooks are never read in entirety, never read from cover to cover. Only small portions are used at any one time. To permit photocopying of these portions is to destroy the use of the books as books."[36] Although publishers are prosperous enough at present to absorb the loss of this market, it is questionable whether they will be able to do so in the future when improved machines will produce copies at progressively lower rates per unit.

The following 1964 figures of the cost to schools per page of printed textbooks and of copying costs are cited by the publishers as indicative of their prospective losses[37]:

	PER PAGE COST
College texts	$.008
High school texts	.006
Elementary school texts	.007
Photocopy of any text	.005

The publishers also note that for schools without copying facilities, Selected Academic Readings, Inc., a firm in New York, will do the job. According to a recent release, the firm offers teachers the opportunity to choose their own readings, and then furnishes these readings in the form of bound books, printed by photo-offset for 2½ cents a page for the first 100 pages, and 2 cents for subsequent pages. (These prices are for a minimum of 100 copies.) For editions of 1,000 copies or more, the prices would be correspondingly lower. "Give educational institutions the right to make multiple copies of extracts without paying for them, and these new devices will drive books of readings and anthologies from the market," comments a publisher.[38]

A brief comment on these figures is warranted. The unit costs for college, high school, and elementary school texts reflect publishers' overhead but it is not clear whether the $.005 cost for a photocopy reflects the cost of the machine, of its operator, rental for the space it occupies, service charges and the time it is inoperative because of some mechanical problem. It should be noted that besides furnishing photocopies at low prices, Selected Academic Readings secures the necessary permission to reprint its materials.

The impact of photocopying upon the market for copyrighted materials was the subject of a study sponsored by the National Science Foundation and conducted by the management consultant firm of George Fry and Associates. The investigators came to the following general conclusions[39]:

1. The author of a scientific or technical journal article finds that it is to his advantage to have his article photoduplicated. Dissemination is in his interest. He suffers no economic damages as he usually receives no compensation for his contribution.

2. Photoduplication of scientific books is extremely limited and takes place only in special circumstances, usually in universities. Industrial and public libraries do hardly any photocopying of books.

3. The circulation of scientific and technical journals has been little affected by photocopying. In order to represent damage to circulation,

a photocopy must be used as a genuine substitute for the journal subscription. There are few instances where this happens.

4. New York Public Library statistics indicate that only 6 percent of all photocopying requests were for journal articles less than one year old. The 150 major corporations involved in the survey, therefore, were hardly substituting photocopies for subscriptions.

5. Where a corporation library depends only on photocopies, there can be economic loss to publishers. Yet the number of times that this occurs in relation to the total picture is so small that it was not considered to be a substantial problem.

6. Sixty percent of the users in the survey ordinarily received the original document directly from their library. Even in large companies, where several hundred research people may be employed, and where several people may be interested in a given article, the librarian frequently routes the single journal to the various individuals involved, rather than produce several individual photocopies.

7. The scientific researcher personally subscribes to two to five journals, exclusive of what the corporation library has.

8. The scientific community in general makes a common practice of exchanging reprints (actually preprints) of articles and this is in fact the most favored means of obtaining a journal article.

9. The majority of journal publishers encourage photoduplication of their articles. The giants of the industry, however, oppose it.

10. The small journal believes that photoduplication actually increases its circulation rather than decreases it, since it makes more people aware of the existence of the less well-known publication. A number of libraries found it more desirable, after seven or eight requests for an article that appeared in a rather obscure journal, to subscribe to the journal rather than to continue ordering photocopies.

In conclusion, the survey on photocopying found that "economic damage does not exist in substance. It does exist in special circumstances, but in relation to the total picture, we do not consider it a major problem."

Publishers question the validity of the survey for these reasons: it was made prior to 1963 and is therefore out of date; it was concerned primarily with photocopying of journals, so that the survey's findings are not applicable to the photocopying of books; and the survey concerned itself mainly with libraries and thus reveals nothing of the photocopying problem in schools.

The American Textbook Publishers Institute subsequently commissioned the National Opinion Research Center (NORC) at the University of Chicago to survey copying practices in schools and colleges in 1965. NORC found several differences between school and college use. On college campuses, photocopying machines are available at many points outside of libraries. Copying is done by librarians, students, and teachers, and the copying from previously published material is considerably greater than in elementary and high schools. The principal sources are journals, monographs, and reference books; in eight of the nineteen colleges surveyed, copies were made for use in the library's reserve collection. Photocopiers in schools, however, were used largely to duplicate a school's administrative materials for administration purposes. When previously published materials were copied, the main sources usually were textbooks, music scores, tests and answer sheets.

The outlook for textbook publishing, however, seems to be brightening. A news item in the New York *Times*[40] revealed that, "With recent increases in federal aid to education, with more students in schools than ever before, and with new technological advances in printing and publishing, sales [of textbooks] are up for the industry as a whole by more than 10 percent this year over the 1965 level. Further and sharper gains are in prospect for next year." A survey of six major companies (Ginn

& Co., Harcourt, Brace & World, Holt, Rinehart & Winston, McGraw-Hill, Prentice-Hall, and Scott, Foresman & Co.) found that their profit margins were significantly higher than they were for the industry as a whole. (There are about 200 companies in the field, and the six major ones account for more than 45 percent of the industry's total revenue.)

Sales of textbooks in 1965 came to $585 million, with elementary school and college sales each accounting for 38 percent of the total, and high school sales for 24 percent.

The article went on to say: "A new factor in the educational field, spurring the use of new types of textbooks and teaching materials, is the rise of automated teaching aides, the use of closed-circuit television and the increased volume of visual aids. These are a considerable help to total volume for the textbook publishers."

So it would seem that despite the uncertainty of the copyright law in reprography, textbook publishing has not been too unprofitable a field.

Even if a librarian or school administrator could determine when the doctrine of fair use applies, and when a report is not in the public domain, how should the copyright holders of materials being photocopied be reimbursed or be paid royalties for the use of their work?

One proposal put forth by the publishers is to license all copying machines. Another is a voluntary licensing system that is based on the purchase of stamps; photocopiers would supply the bibliographical information on cards to be sent to a central agency. It is not too clear how the concepts of fair use and public domain enter into the charge for stamps, and librarians particularly question the workability of this system.

A proposal that has aroused some enthusiasm among publishers is a copyright clearinghouse, i.e., a system, modeled after ASCAP, under which publishers would voluntarily list their works with a clearinghouse, which then would license copying services to copy the listed works. Payments to publishers would be based on a sampling of the works copied. There would be a modest charge for the copying service, and the fair-use doctrine would not be pertinent.

To suggest the difficulties a clearinghouse system would encounter in trying to collect royalties for photoduplicating, it is worth while to review the misgivings recently voiced by a representative of an authors' organization.

"All royalties collected annually [would have to be distributed] among the thousands of authors and publishers whose works are copied, on a sampling and averaging basis. While this may be suitable to the licensing of public performances of music, it would not be feasible for the types of uses that occur in the copying medium. ASCAP [which uses] the sampling and averaging approach, collects the bulk of its income by licensing radio and television stations, its principle customers, on a gross fee basis–fees based on the broadcasters' gross receipts. Obviously, licenses could not be issued on this basis in the copying medium.

"True, it is possible that license fees could be paid for each copying without any accompanying information and in that event a sampling approach would have to be used. But could it work? ASCAP samples performances, i.e., keeps records of representative numbers of performances of its members' compositions on a comparatively few radio and television stations throughout the United States and from these projects the total number of performances each composition was likely to have had. These are *public* performances; they are checked by turning on a radio or television set. Copying is not public; and the number of users could be many times greater. Accurate sampling would be much more difficult; the projection might be harmful to individual authors.

"Moreover, the sampling and averaging approach is complex–ASCAP takes other factors than number of uses into account. It is costly, possibly much more so than the cost of distributing royalties on a per-use basis. And, it is far from acceptable to all concerned; it produces considerable controversy as to whether various composers and publishers are receiving their fair share of the pool of royalties."[41]

Needless to say, librarians and educators are less than enthusiastic about a clearinghouse licensing system or any other system suggested by the publishers for photocopying permission. The exorbitant costs involved in such a permission-and-payment system are bothersome even to the publishers. As Benjamin observed some time ago:

"Everyone who has looked into the problem of establishing a comprehensive system for permission and payments knows that the difficulty of its solution lies in the two words 'cheap' and 'easy.' Personally, I doubt that any easy system can be devised to operate cheaply. Yet almost everyone who talks about paying publishers for reproduction rights speaks only of 'nominal' fees. When one examines proposed systems for charging, accounting, paying and receiving fees, and for dividing them with authors (as must be done, of course), one always finds that the publishers would be paying nickles and dimes to collect pennies. Naturally, this prospect does not engage our enthusiasm nor arouse us to action."[42] The answer, he believes, may lie in the payment of substantial rather than nominal fees–substantial enough to absorb the cost of the system–or in a government subsidy of a million dollars or more annually.

An alternative scheme would provide for a flat percentage royalty to be paid by the federal government from a tax levied on the gross receipts of copying-machine operators, with a requirement that records be kept of the items copied. But this, too, has been met with disapproval by the community of scholars as well as by the hardware people.

While a commercial statute or a statutorily granted legal cause of action (with minimum damages set) are possible remedies for copying in violation of copyright, they probably would not be very effective in practice, since a) juries would be reluctant to convict, b) it would be difficult to decide who the guilty party was—the library, the person making the copy, or the person for whom the copy was made, and c) it would be difficult to know when such copying was taking place.

Why is so much copying being done at present? Charles P. Yerkes, sales director at Microcard Corp., has some interesting thoughts on this subject. There is an incredible amount of printed information available today and it seems to be doubling every ten years. Also there is an increasing need for quick information; time spent in reducing information to a usable, convenient form is time wasted for the researcher. Furthermore, the scientist or engineer needs ideas from others to form his own. This, Yerkes points out, is one of the anomalies of copying. "The researcher, student, scientist, or engineer does not really want the copy he has. . . . He is fundamentally looking for ideas. The fact that it is on a piece of paper in this particular form could not matter less to him. He is looking for ideas within the paper." Increased use of copying also reflects the fact that there are more scientists and engineers today than ever before.[43]

But there is also a considerable amount of copying going on for reasons of style, content, information, and arrangement, just as a considerable portion of the copying activities reflects duplication of non-copyrighted materials or copying under conditions the fair-use doctrine would allow.

The question is how the contending parties react to the implications arising from the mechanical and electronic reproduction of copyrighted materials. Scholars and educators look upon all proposals for obtaining permission to copy copyrighted materials for use in schools, colleges, and libraries as unnecessary nuisances, and are irked by controls that would affect their non-profit motivation. The publishers, by their own admission, have responded slowly, if not "apathetically." They seem to be aware of the need to move beyond their position but are undecided in what direction. Unfortunately, the publishers and the educational community are strongly opposed to each other—to an extent that Congressman Emanuel Celler, in summarizing the Congressional Hearings of 1964, felt compelled to complain:

"Perhaps the most perplexing issue facing you involves the permissible limits of educational copying. . . . I am advised that the publishers and authors on the one side and the educational groups on the other have now dug in and are engaged in positional or trench warfare. . . . I believe that you will neither ignore the need of teachers for access to educational material without undue fuss, nor will you accept the thesis that authors, as a class, must subsidize education. But, it is to be hoped that the subcommittee will not have to make the entire decision itself, for the publishers and authors on the one hand and the teachers on the other both agree that they are indispensable to each other, and the issue seems to me to be eminently negotiable."[44]

But with the protagonists in "entrenched" positions, how can the photocopying problem be solved? It appears to the author of this report that the solution lies with the publishers and not the consumers, for several reasons:

1. A greatly improved technology and new sources of capital offer publishers an opportunity to initiate imaginative changes in their mode of operation. "If publishing and journalism do not buy automation, automation will buy them," warns Charles M. Stevens of INTREX. "Computer costs will virtually vanish. . . . If publishers experiment now with computers and advanced technology, they will be an important part of the future instead of its victim." Publishers will have to learn to live with the new technology and to use it for their own ends instead of permitting the hardware people to supplant them. Above all, pub-

lishers must try to find a solution to the new technology within the framework of the open market.

2. Copyright infringement by photocopying is not as bad as the statistics would indicate. While large industrial companies and libraries are among the principal users, they are also purchasing many new titles and journal subscriptions (as well as keeping old ones) to have bibliographical control over the articles they want to circulate. It should be recognized too that a company would never maintain a journal subscription for, say, 40 or 400 copies merely because there once was a demand for that many copies of a given article. It is doubtful, furthermore, whether a journal could supply the additional copies, as scientific magazines are often printed in relatively small editions.

There is much private and casual copying by students, faculty and others in college and university libraries, since students rarely buy books other than those assigned by the instructor, i.e., they rarely buy extracurricular readings. If they were deprived of the opportunity to photocopy those readings, they would merely wait their turn for one of the reserved copies. Nor will a library depend on only one copy of a publication assigned by an instructor. The purchasing pattern in all libraries reflects the size of the budget, the available space, the number of students involved, and the interest in specific publications. At a certain point the librarian has to decide how many copies he has to buy to balance these various interests. Thereafter, the exigencies of meeting student demand take over. It is here where the student either waits his turn to read an assigned book or article on reserve, or makes a photocopy of the pages he deems important. Rarely does a library buy enough copies of a book to provide for the needs of all students. If the demand persists, the library may photocopy a journal article, but not too often a book—certainly never in such amounts as to create alarm. As a matter of fact, librarians are not happy with the photocopying of library materials, for books and periodicals are often badly abused and the need to replace or rebind them is accelerated.

3. The cost of photocopying in libraries and schools, even with Xerox machines, is not as low as it appears. If a library employee who earns $2 an hour must be away from his assigned position for about five to ten minutes to take a shot of a page (the time spent in locating an article or book, walking to the photocopier, heating it up, etc.), it costs the institution between 17 and 33 cents to make that photocopy. If a full-time operator is employed for this purpose, it may cost the institution from $75 to $100 a week in salary. Demand is irregular and may not always be sufficient to keep the machine operating at all times. When the photocopier breaks down, the operator is idle for a day or two. And the rental or purchasing cost of the machine will also have to be considered.

Another fact to remember is that researchers, scholars, and academicians rarely buy the books they use in their research. They receive complimentary copies, review or desk copies, and reprints of articles, or they borrow library copies. Only if these sources fail to provide the materials sought, do they resort to photocopying. The publishers' complaint that photocopying is depriving them of profits because of lost sales may therefore not be a completely valid conclusion. Many of the potential sales the publishers envision are not of the type that ordinarily occurs. It may well be, that the publisher, despite all this photocopying, is no worse off than before.

4. Copying for instructional purposes in the classroom is also subject to the logistics of the problem, and here is where the publishers can take the initiative. The use of microforms and other machine-readable forms, for example, is sure to increase. There is no reason why the publisher should not take advantage of this tremendous growth in "non-book" publishing, instead of leaving this market to the hardware people.

With the available modern technology, publishers should be able to provide, on a competitive basis, copies of the excerpts of their publications required by the schools. The filmstrips, charts, chapters, or pages of books, and the reprints of articles could all be supplied by the publishers on a cost-plus-royalty basis low enough to encourage or entice school districts to purchase multiple copies rather than photocopy them. If University Microfilms can offer demand publishing at 5 cents a page, including the cost of clearance of rights, there is no reason why publishers cannot do the same with their own publications, or do it even more economically. Eugene Power, chairman of University Microfilms, is certain that demand publishing–i.e., the production of books only after they have been ordered–will gain an important place in the book industry, particularly since it relieves the publisher of storage costs and remainder losses. Power points out that "if 300 books are required, they can be produced one at a time at the same price as if they were printed on an offset press."

To arrange for this service, the publishers should issue catalogues of their books and list the cost for copies by page or chapter, in bulk sales or otherwise. Bobbs-Merrill & Co. is using this system at present to sell reprints of law review articles. New books could list such price information on the verso of the title page.

Publishers may want to establish cooperative regional offices to service these requests or develop other alternative systems. Eventually, these systems would link up with computer storage and retrieval units that would provide practically instantaneous transmission in remote, ephemeral, or hard-copy form. They could also provide microforms if requested. Once the dissemination of copy is centralized, a logical solution to the photocopying problem is possible.

Publishers claim that the consumer is becoming a publisher by the use of photocopying machines. One way to remedy this is for the publishers to establish an improved publishing service that will provide photocopies and service at a competitive rate. Some publishers are aware of this opportunity and their mergers with companies in the communications industry are indicative of future cooperation.

Librarians and the educational community would prefer to cooperate with the publishing industry. They would not choose photocopying if publishers would offer a service that met their needs. But it is precisely because the publishers have failed to meet these needs (perhaps they never thought of copying as one of the services they could provide at a profit) that the problem has been created. Robert K. Kunnath, a librarian at Wayne State University, reflected the educational community's feelings when he said: "If a reprint is available, we'd rather buy it from the publisher than make it ourselves."[45]

The Information Explosion and the New Technology

> "Just as the first copyright laws were a response to an earlier revolution brought on by the development of the printing press, so must a copyright statute today respond to the challenge of a technology based on instant communication and reproduction of an author's works throughout the world."[46]

This appraisal by the Register of Copyrights suggests the problems the intellectual community is facing as a result of the technological revolution in communications. A major concern of the current information explosion is the identification, processing, storage and retrieval of information, which may in very short time become obsolete. As a result of the need for rapid retrieval, a technological breakthrough of such dimensions has occurred that there is a question whether the traditional copyright rules are still applicable.

A primary need of the present-day society is accessibility to information, past and present, copyrighted, as well as in the public domain. To achieve this objective it is necessary to take advantage of the tremendous potential of the new technology as well as of the more prosaic, traditional communication media. Ways and means will have to be found to disseminate this information and still protect the developers' interests. It would appear that the right of access to information would have to be weighed against the economic incentives of creators to continue creating. But the private creators who are seeking protection for their works also need to have immediate and unlimited access to the information that is being developed by the research community in order to continue creating.

The information explosion is also changing the traditional tools of research. The library of the future will be unrecognizable to the librarian of today; it will be so dependent on the hardware of the new technology, that, apocryphally speaking, the librarian of the future will be a mechanic with a screwdriver, ever alert to repair breakdowns in the service.

Because of the need to master tremendous masses of information in interrelated disciplines, the entrepreneur researcher will give way to the research team. Not only will collaboration become characteristic of intellectual research, but there will also be a greater dependence on the products created by the computer programs.

Researchers, professional librarians, and educators are already involved with the new techniques of electronic document-storage and computerized information-retrieval systems, and are gradually learning the exciting possibilities of miniaturization and remote transmission of data. The following predictions and speculations indicate some of these possibilities:

1. "There is . . . no technical obstacle in principle, and probably none of an economic kind either, why I should not be able to dial a roll of microfilm in a London library, have some pages transmitted to me [in Washington, D.C.] by telefacsimile, and pay for the service on my telephone bill."[47]

2. "In the university of the future, as it is visualized at M.I.T., the library will be the central facility of an information-transfer network that will extend throughout the academic community. Students and scholars will use this network to gain access to the university's total information resources, through Touch-Tone telephones, teletypewriter keyboards, television-like displays, and quickly made copies. The users of the system will communicate with each other as well as with the library; data just obtained in the laboratory and comments made by observers will be as easily available as the texts of books in the library or documents in the departmental files. The information traffic will be controlled by means of the university's time-shared computer utility, much as today's verbal communications are handled by the campus telephone exchange. Long-distance service will connect the university's information-transfer network with sources and users elsewhere. . . .

"The traditional library provides access by lending the original document, but that method is incompatible with the principle of guaranteed access, which should govern the information-transfer systems of the future. We must find ways of providing transient or permanent access that do not preclude the concurrent access to the same document by other users of the system.

"The loan of duplicate copies, in either full size or microform, is a possible technique. Other important possibilities are visual displays on optical or electronic screens.

"For permanent . . . access, full-size paper copies are the most obvious solution. Such copies can be made directly from the original document, or they can be derived from microform copies of the original. They can be produced at a distance by signals transmitted over electrical circuits. . . . Permanent copies might also be supplied to users in reduced size, either on paper or on film."[48]

3. "We believe that the total library holdings of all of our 58 cam-

puses [State University of New York] can one day be made available to every faculty member and to every student on every campus [through the communication sciences].

"We believe that with a communications network an interchange of teaching resources and research ideas can be effected....

"We believe that some learning can be accomplished by computer-assisted instruction, thereby freeing the student and the faculty member for a more vital kind of interaction. We believe closed circuit inter-campus television conferences can be taped, stored, and transmitted at will over the educational broadcasting system. We believe that tele-facsimile and computerized print-outs make feasible the prospect of study terminals located in dormitories, in apartments, in libraries, and in student unions, so that the stored resources of the institution and its fact-transmitting system can be available 24 hours a day throughout the entire University."[49]

4. "The medical libraries of three major eastern universities will be tied together in a network of computers and telephone lines to give scholars virtually instant access to their pooled resources... the three libraries will then contain 1,025,000 items. These can be searched by computers in seconds.... When telecommunication and photographic reproducing devices are added to the network system... pages from a book in New York could be flashed to a user in another city and even reproduced for him in take-home form."[50]

5. "You must imagine, at the eventual heart of things to come, linked or integrated systems of networks of computers, capable of storing faithful simulacra of the entire treasure of the accumulated knowledge and artistic production of past ages, and of taking into the store new intelligence of all sorts as produced. The systems will have a prodigious capacity for manipulating the store in useful ways, for selecting portions of it upon call and transmitting them at any distance, where they

will be converted as desired to forms, directly or indirectly cognizable—whether as printed pages, phono records, tapes, transient displays of sights or sounds, or hieroglyphs for further machine uses. Lasers, microwave channels, satellites improving on Comsat's Early Bird, and no doubt, many devices now unnamable, will operate as ganglions to extend the reach of the systems to the ultimate users as well as to provide a copious array of additional services."[51]

6. A statistical study by the American Federation of Information Processing Societies (AFIPS) reveals that computer equipment presently in use in the U.S. is valued at more than $7.8 billion. Projections indicate the value of this equipment will approximate $18 billion by 1970, and $31.5 billion by 1975, when an established 85,000 computers will be in use. Today's computers are more than 900 times faster than the 1950 models. A program running an hour on a 1950 computer would take only three to four seconds on today's high-speed computer. The survey also notes that of the total investment in programing and software, presently estimated at $1.5 billion a year, *75 percent is being spent by the computer manufacturers.*[52]

How will these new developments affect copyright law and the protection of intellectual property? There are several possibilities:

1. Intellectual team effort may eventually affect the copyright concept of providing an incentive for entrepreneur creators.

2. The integrity of a basic collection of materials, miniaturized or compacted and stored in electronic information-center computers, will be preserved by xerographic printers providing facsimile reproduction by remote transmission in hard-copy form, or by video scanning of ephemeral copy on a closed-circuit TV monitor elsewhere. The collection remains intact because the computer, in essence, assumes the role of a duplicating rather than a circulating library. One copy of a book fed into such a system can service all simultaneous demands for it; of

course, this substitution for additional copies will vitally affect the publishers' traditional market.

3. Microfiches and computer print-outs will probably replace copyrighted hard-copy publication of research reports as well as of scientific and technical materials currently appearing in journals, monographs, and books.

4. Products created by electronically computerized information systems will necessitate a new method of compensation. And what kind of recognition should be accorded them as intellectual property?

5. Audio-visual dial-access teaching machines, operated by remote control, will provide hundreds and even thousands of students with simultaneous audio and visual access to a journal article or excerpts from a book. This in turn will necessitate a new approach to the copyright laws, one which will have to consider the requirements of the creator of the book or the information, the consumer, the communication medium, and the original publisher.

Some copyright experts, like attorney John Schulman, believe that there is nothing incompatible between the copyright law and the proper use of computer techniques for the cataloguing and retrieving of information. "The question of propriety arises essentially in respect of the form in which data is stored and retrieved, and the form in which it is ultimately disseminated."[53]

Copyright "rights" pertain to an author's exclusive right to copy or perform his works; they do not protect *ideas* but rather the expression and style in which the ideas have been presented. There is nothing in the copyright law that denies the public the use of concepts or facts brought out in the copyrighted materials. For this reason Schulman believes that copyright, "rather than being a detriment to computer technology, may, in fact, provide an affirmative boon to those who devote their efforts to that activity." The concept of fair use will permit proper extraction of ideas and of their expression for use in computers and Schulman therefore feels that the copyright law "does not impede or prevent the proper utilization of material for storage and retrieval purposes." He concludes: "Although computer technology may be novel, its copyright problems are not entirely new. They were solved in principle long before the advent of electronic data storage and retrieval. Those who deal with these newer methods of processing and programming need only follow the same rules and procedures, and exercise the same restraints which are observed by the publishers of books and periodicals. If these liberal roles are adhered to, the copyright system will not constitute a threat or a road block to progress."

Other experts, however, are not so certain that the copyright law is explicit enough to cope with the new technology. One of the most persistent problems is to determine at what point an infringement occurs. Bella Linden, another attorney and copyright expert, describes some of the situations with which lawyers are now struggling.[54] In the main they are instances where the copyright owner has not consented to the use of his literary property in the computer, either by way of input, storage, or output. "Input and storage, even at the present state of the art, are achieved via a variety of means, such as: key-word indexing; conceptual abstracting; special electric typewriting; punch cards; microfilm; magnetic tape, and devices capable of capturing electronic impulses." Mrs. Linden brings out that, aside from the question of whether conceptual indexing and abstracting violate the rights of the copyright holder or are subject to the doctrine of fair use, "the basic rights susceptible of infringement by computer usage appear to be the 'copying' and 'performance' rights. Output or retrieval of the copyrighted work may be in the form of abstracts, excerpts, or the work as a whole. It may be delivered to the user in tangible form such as a photoduplication or in ephemeral form such as the temporary projection of an image on the screen. Thus, the information may be captured and disseminated by computers in tangible or intangible, ephemeral or visually perceivable form."

Committees No. 304 and No. 408 of the Patent, Trademark, and Copyright Section of the American Bar Association are not in agreement on how to treat the output or end product of a computer process. Committee No. 408 recommends, "The output of an information storage and retrieval system should not be considered a copyright infringement or derivative work if such output is an index, abstract, limited quotation or analysis of the copyrighted work, except to the extent that the output is likely to diminish the demand for the copyrighted work." Committee No. 304 insists that the doctrine of fair use should govern in this case. The situation is aggravated when the output is a visual image or, as may happen, a performance rather than hard copy. The Register of Copyrights has commented on this possibility of "showing, rather than distributing, copies as a means of disseminating an author's work. In addition to improved projection equipment, the use of closed-and-open-circuit television for presenting images of graphic and textual material to large audiences of spectators, could, in the near future, have drastic effects upon copyright owners' rights. Equally if not more significant for the future are the implications of information storage and retrieval devices; when linked together by communication satellites or other means, these could eventually provide libraries and individuals throughout the world with access to a single copy of a work by transmission of electronic images. It is not inconceivable that in certain areas at least, 'exhibition' may take over from 'reproduction' of 'copies' as the means of presenting authors' works to the public, and we are now convinced that a basic right of public exhibition should be expressly recognized in the statute."[55] Here again, however, the copyright law and even its proposed revision are not too clear on where an infringement occurs in these situations.

Mrs. Linden notes that the term "copy" is a word of art construed by the courts to mean a copy which is "visually perceivable" and in "tangible form." She wonders whether, when we are concerned with computer output of punch cards or tape, we are "copying" or, in fact, performing the copyright owner's property publicly? This is not too clear and Mrs. Linden cautions: "If the computer system's uses of information protected under [the copyright law] are construed neither as the making of copies nor as performances of the work in whole or in part, then such uses, no matter how injurious to the pecuniary interests of the copyright proprietor (absent fair use), are uses which appear to be unprotected by the Copyright Act. On the other hand, a contrary construction, which can find equal support, would accord protection to the copyright proprietor even in some cases where the computer processes have not produced a 'copy' of the work."

It would appear therefore that the application of the law of copyright to the techniques of information and retrieval processes is not so concise as to be acceptable to all copyright experts. Aside from the fact that it is almost impossible to determine when a computer system has infringed on a copyright owner's literary property or for that matter to what extent, legal experts do not agree on whether the copyright law can provide for all the new uses of copyrighted material that the new technology has developed. It is not clear either whether the principles of "unfair competition" on the ground of "passing off" one's work or product as another's would be applicable as a substitute where the copyright law cannot protect the copyright proprietor.

The experts cannot even agree on whether the mere unlicensed conversion of a copyrighted work into computer readable form should be considered an infringement. The Register of Copyright believes it is an infringement because storage in a computer system is either a "reproduction" or a "derivative" work. The ABA's Committee No. 408, however, favors the application of the fair-use doctrine to allow the use of copyrighted works in information storage and retrieval systems in accordance with the following principles:

1. The conversion of a copyrighted work into computer readable form by other than the copyright proprietor for use in the converter's information and storage retrieval systems should be considered a fair use, unless the author or copyright proprietor has copyrighted such a conversion and makes it available for information storage and retrieval use upon reasonable terms.

2. The mere storage in a computer memory of a copyrighted work or of a work derived therefrom whether directly or through a computer readable conversion should not be considered an infringement, except to the extent that the information storage and retrieval system output is an infringement.

On the other hand, Committee No. 304 of the same ABA section opposes this view, objecting to the granting of special exemptions. It denies any statutory exemptions in such a situation, "except to the extent that the use in any specific case falls within the doctrine of fair use as the same is generally applicable to other permissible unauthorized uses of copyrighted works." Benjamin Kaplan of the Harvard University Law School contends that infringement should not turn on input conversion but rather on output conversion—on what is subsequently done with the stored work. "Print-outs of the work would be analagous to photocopies," he reasons, "but suppose the print-out is merely an index or short resumé, taking nothing substantial from the work; suppose the work is merely exhibited by the volume to its clients in circumstances which would otherwise constitute an exempt occasion? The Register evidently believes copying for storage must be controlled because the machines are capable of a great variety of uses and outputs, but it is not apparent to me that the Register's blanket proposal is prudent at the present stage of computer development, or sound for the long future."[56]

There are other copyright problems brought out by the new technology. For example, the requirements in the copyright law of notice of copyright and deposit do not apply to the dissemination of unpublished manuscripts fed into information storage and retrieval systems. Questions arise as to when the manuscript has been published by the computer, especially when only parts of it appear at a time in the output. It is even questionable whether the doctrine of fair use is applicable to photocopying and computer devices. In her testimony before Subcommittee No. 3 on Copyright Law Revision, Mrs. Linden was asked by Congressman Edward Hutchinson whether the publishers' proposal for blanket licensing as a solution for use of copyrighted materials in photocopying devices and computer systems would not supersede the doctrine of fair use:

(Mrs. Linden): "No. I don't believe so, because I really do not think the doctrine of fair use is applicable . . . there is not a single case . . . where the doctrine of fair use has been tested with respect to the reprinting of even the smallest portion of a copyrighted work by a Xerox or some other photocopying device.

"It is my view, and I believe it is shared by many, that the doctrine of fair use was developed to take care of literary criticism, to the copying by longhand of an inconsequential portion of a work, even though that latter is technically a copyright infringement, because the author, under our present section 1, has exclusive copying rights."[57]

The computerized retrieval process is difficult to monitor. Assuming that the copyright law is adequate to protect the rights of copyright proprietors in literary works converted into machine storage and retrieval, detection of any possible infringement would be an almost insurmountable obstacle to adequate control. For this reason, it is the reasoning of Committee No. 304 that "the complete freedom to copy for storage purposes, and the right to retrieve portions of copyrighted works without incurring liability for infringement, would of necessity impair, if not destroy completely, the benefits of copyright in the works which were used for these purposes."

To indicate some of the problems involved in this respect, Committee 304 suggests considering the possible answers to the following questions:

Would the exemption be available to the following:

1. Individuals and companies engaged in the business of translating or converting copyrighted material into computer readable form who offer these translations and conversions or copies thereof for sale to the public.
2. Individuals or companies engaged in the business of preparing translations or conversions for the account of owners, lessees, or operators of storage and retrieval systems.
3. Individuals or companies engaged in the business of reproducing copyrighted works on tape, disks, microfilm or other such devices for use by the operators of storage and retrieval systems.
4. Individuals or companies who lease computers or provide computer service to the public.

Would this exemption apply to:

1. All kinds of copyrighted material, including literary and dramatic works, musical compositions, motion pictures and artistic works.
2. Sound recordings and other works produced on film, tape or wire.
3. Copyrighted works originally published in one species of computer readable language, when converted or translated into another species of computer readable language.

If the output of the retrieval processes were to exceed the limits of fair use who, among the following, would be liable for infringement and to what extent would each of them be liable?

1. The converter or translator of the original material into machine readable language, the purchaser or other person who acquires the converted product for the computer device, the owner, lessee, or operator of the computer, the owner or operator of the computer service establishments, the recipient of the output, or the person who prints or publishes the material retrieved.

2. Would the copyright proprietor be entitled to protect himself against a continuation or a repetition of the infringement by enjoining the further use of the copyrighted material in its translated or converted form or any other form in which it had been stored.

3. If by successive print-outs or retrievals of portions of the work, the copyrighted work were reproduced in its entirety, would the copyright proprietor be entitled to protection.

Failure to meet these special contingencies by statute, the committee holds, would result in "endless controversy and litigation." Rather than destroy the rights of authors and other creators by such an exemption (freedom to use copyrighted material in an information and retrieval system without authorization, as provided in the resolution of Committee No. 408), Committee No. 304 recommends that more study and thought be given to "the establishment of clearinghouses by which the issuance of licenses might be expedited and simplified." A clearinghouse licensing system would be "more logical and equitable to all parties concerned, and more in keeping with the public interest than the establishment of special exemptions favoring the users of specific devices." All unauthorized users of copyrighted works who would not submit to such a licensing system would be bound by the application of the fair-use doctrine.

The legal problems outlined above with reference to computerized research (and there are others that are also worthy of consideration) highlight the difficulties involved in reconciling the interests of the public (scholars, researchers, etc.) in freely utilizing ideas and information expressed in literary works with the need to encourage researchers and authors to create works. The present copyright law has accomplished this reconciliation by granting "exclusive" rights to authors and permitting the unauthorized use of their works under the principle of fair use. The proposed revision of the copyright law incorporates both these approaches, setting forth authors' rights and then expressly providing for exemptions that would not be considered an infringement of these rights. Specific exemptions are allowed in "face to face" teaching, non-profit educational broadcasting intended primarily for classroom reception as part of a teaching program, religious services, and performances for some educational, religious, and charitable purposes. The revision also provides that "fair use of a copyrighted work is not an infringement of copyright."

The proposed draft of the new copyright law, however, still leaves much ground for contention. One great obstacle to a reasonable solution lies in the difficulty of identifying the novel uses that will be made of copyrighted materials by the new technology—or for that matter, identifying the rights that the copyright proprietor should be granted to encourage him to create. The ATPI position, for example, is that more is involved here than the right to scan copyrighted works lawfully programed into the memory core of a computer system for the purpose of selecting appropriate sections. The copyright law must provide for the concept of the "non-book"—a literary work that is not in perceivable or tangible form—which is subject, through the new technology, to wide distribution, dissemination, and use. The ATPI is concerned that, although the draft of the proposed copyright-law bill protects the copyright proprietor from unauthorized input into the computer, etc., it does not consider the implications of the next stage—i.e., computer scanning that selects relevant portions of a copyrighted work for retrieval either in hard copy or ephemeral form. The ATPI is particularly concerned that "images flashed on screens" are now taking the place of copies printed on paper as a means of using an author's works.

Publishers and authors are speculating about the large electronically computerized storage and information systems that will be developed in the near future. How will they affect commercial publishing when they become as much a part of the national scene as the telephone? Are they a threat to survival or a promise of even greater achievements? It is obvious that when it comes to protection of intellectual property, information retrieval will be the point of departure rather than document retrieval. People in the copyright area have been accused of being confused about photocopying machines, computers, and document storage. The Xerox process is comparatively cheap but difficult to control. Computers are different: they can be programed to retrieve documents either ephemerally or in hard copy, directly or by remote transmission. They can be programed to retrieve information abstracted and selected from these documents. They can accommodate and arrange these documents in an orderly and logical program that will retrieve for the user answers to questions addressed to the facility. Sophisticated and complicated information programs can be fed into computers with apparent ease. They can be linked and made compatible with other information systems in a regional pattern and the regional programs in turn can be linked with compatible national and even international programs through the Early Bird or other satellite relay transmissions. The speed of information transfer will determine the thrust of this development. All that is required to develop these systems is time, capital, and the need for a program. The technical knowledge and competence are already available. But most important, computers can be controlled. Thus, if the technology of the future does not respond to the traditional copyright rules, the computer will have to be programed to provide substitute incentives for creators, as well as to allow for the free flow of knowledge.

The information world of the future will revolve around information systems, educational programs, and library complexes in which the complete documentation of the system concerned will be equivalent to a computer memory. In a sense, therefore, by providing copies of works stored in the computer, these systems become publishers. Traditional publications will also be available from commercial publishers, but it would seem that "non-book" production will predominate. As a result, the role of the commercial publisher will probably change, especially in his relationship with authors and readers. Publishers will also have to reconsider the role they will want to play with reference to the regional and national information networks the government is planning and developing. Similarly, libraries will have to readjust their concepts of reader's service and technical operations. Libraries eventually will also become part of the projected government information networks. As recently as September 2, 1966, President Johnson named a commission to study ways of improving the nation's libraries. In announcing its creation he explained that he had asked the commission "to appraise the role and adequacy of our libraries, now and in the future, as sources for scholarly research, as centers for the distribution of knowledge, as links in our nation's rapidly evolving communications networks."

It would appear, therefore, that the technological breakthrough will change the concept of author protection, and that copyright protection will be of little significance to the author of scholarly works. Rather than depend on royalties, he will seek other avenues of compensation. The market for traditional publication of his work will be so limited, that unless his product is of extraordinary merit and importance, he would sell it directly to the information-system operator. As in traditional publishing, an author could arrange for an outright sale or for an accounting, but the latter would be based on use rather than on sales. In this situation, therefore, copyright protection would serve no purpose, even if it were available to the author. The scholarly work could be quickly programed into the system and retrieved in hard copy, or ephemerally by remote transmission, or converted into information sought by the user of the system. Sophisticated accounting details could be fed into the system to account for use of the work according to a pre-arranged scale of rates. Operators of computer systems are certain that this can be done. Users of the systems will probably consist of subscribers paying fixed rates for standard services and additional charges for extraordinary services, or casual users paying prescribed rates according to a classified scale. In library complexes the users ordinarily will be students, teachers and researchers. Computerized library systems in universities will probably charge students a so-called "library fee" to maintain the service, or include such a charge in the tuition fee. Special arrangements could be made with faculty members and researchers seeking access to the university computers' memory. Similar arrangements could be made for the use of regional as well as national and international systems.

Inasmuch as the local setup would be centrally administered, it will be possible to construct a licensing system that obtains clearance for the copyrighted materials fed into it. Clearinghouses could be established for this purpose. As the copyright expires on these materials, the computer will be programed to take advantage of it. As timeliness will be of the essence, it will probably be more profitable for proprietors of copyrighted works to negotiate a special deal for their computer use than to depend on traditional royalties.

Of course, this development will be accompanied by many problems. Government interests, for example, will have to be protected, especially in the area of national security. Serious questions will also arise as to the amount of control the government should have over these information systems. Should they be treated as public utilities, perhaps, and be regulated by the government as other communication media are? Should rates established by the networks or information systems be subject to antitrust legislation? International agreements and treaties will have to be negotiated to ensure flawless transmission of information.

Some publishers, recognizing the handwriting on the wall, are preparing for the future by merging with electronic companies. But they will have to change their mode of operations radically if they want to survive. Laborers are being warned that they will not get tomorrow's jobs with today's skills. Publishers should take notice of this admonition.

As to the authors' incentive to create, it is possible that information-system operators will make their own contracts with the authors and ask them to prepare their works especially for dissemination through the computer. Most of the materials will probably be developed through team effort, a method of researching and writing that will change the author's psychological need to identify with his work and to promote his professional image. Finally, it should be remembered that the machine itself will eventually be so programed that it too can claim authorship of original works.

Footnotes

1. Vol. 30, No. 144, p. 9408-9409.
2. Price, *Government and Science*. New York: Oxford University Press, 1962, p. 86.
3. The Massachusetts Institute of Technology derives a sum four times greater than its normal school budget from federal research. Columbia University acknowledges that one-half of its budget depends on federal contracts and grants. Federal support accounted for 84 percent of the total funds expended in research at New York University during the period 1964-65.
4. Barber, *The Politics of Research*. Washington: Public Affairs Press, 1966, p. 32.
5. The New York *Times*, August 21, 1966, p. 49.
6. *American Education*, November 1965, p. 7ff.
7. U.S. *Congress, Senate, Committee on Labor and Public Welfare*, Higher Education Act of 1965. Hearings, 89th Congress, 1st session, p. 1407ff.
8. S. 789; S. 1809. 89th Congress, 1st session.
9. *Editor and Publisher*, September 2, 1961, p. 64.
10. U.S. *Congress, House, Committee on the Judiciary*, Copyright Law Revision. Hearings, 89th Congress, 1st session, p. 1922.
11. Price, *op. cit.*, p. 92.
12. Benjamin, *Copyright or Public Domain?* 1965, no pagination.
13. Supplementary Report of the Register of Copyrights on the General Revision of the U.S. Copyright Law: 1965 Revision Bill, p. 9-10.

14. U.S. *Congress, House, op. cit.,* p. 1559.

15. American Council of Learned Societies, *Newsletter,* December 1965.

16. U.S. *Congress, Senate, op. cit.,* p. 780ff.

17. *Ibid.,* p. 1413.

18. *Congressional Record,* February 1, 1965, p. 1670.

19. *Congressional Record,* January 28, 1965, p. 1497.

20. *Ibid.,* p. 1499.

21. Goodlad, *The Changing School Curriculum.* New York: The Fund for Advancement of Education, 1966, p. 11-19.

22. U.S. *Congress, House, op. cit.,* p. 66ff.

23. Benjamin, *op. cit.*

24. *Science,* January 21, 1966, p. 281.

25. *The Development of a Sequential and Cumulative Program in English for Able College-Bound Students in Senior High School, Grades 10 Through 12.*

26. *PMLA,* September 1964, part 2, p. 54.

27. Howe, *Education and the Changing Technology.* Speech delivered at Conference on "Engineering Systems for Education and Training," Arlington, Va., June 14, 1966, p. 9.

28. *Science, Government, and Information.* A Report of the President's Science Advisory Committee. Washington: The White House, January 10, 1963, p. 20-21.

29. Hattery, *Federal Programs and Commercial Book Publishing* (mimeo). January 25, 1966, p. 150.

30. American Library Association, *The Library and Information Networks of the Future.* Prepared for the Rome Air Development Center, Air Force Systems Command, U.S. Air Force, Rome, N. Y.: Griffiss Air Force Base, 1963, p. 21.

31. The New York *Times,* April 10, 1966, p. 55.

32. Burchinal and Haswell, "How to Put Two and a Half Tons of Research Into One Handy Little Box." *American Education,* February 1966, p. 23ff.

33. Barber, *op. cit.,* p. 91.

34. U.S. *Congress, House, op. cit.,* p. 1859-1860.

35. Folsom v. March, 9 Fed. Cas. 342 (CCD Mass.).

36. ATPI statement submitted to Senator McClellan on October 29, 1965. *The Case Against the Proposed Section 111 Amendment to S. 1006* (mimeo), p. 16.

37. *Ibid.*, p. 25.

38. *Ibid.*, p. 25-26.

39. Hattery and Bush (eds.), *Reprography and Copyright Law.* Baltimore: Port City Press, Inc., 1964, p. 52.

40. The New York *Times,* August 28, 1966, sect. 3, p. 1.

41. Karp, "A 'Statutory' Licensing System for the Limited Copying of Copyrighted Works." *Bulletin of the Copyright Society of the U.S.A.*, February 1965, p. 203-204.

42. Hattery and Bush (eds.), *op. cit.*, p. 110.

43. *Ibid.*, p. 71-72.

44. U.S. *Congress, House, op. cit.*, p. 1854-1855.

45. *Publishers Weekly,* August 1, 1966, p. 40.

46. U.S. *Congress, Senate, Committee on the Judiciary,* Copyright Law Revision. Hearings, 89th Congress, 1st session, August 18, 1965.

47. Clapp, "Closing the Circuit." *Library Journal,* March 1, 1966, p. 1170.

48. Overhage, "Plans for Project Intrex." *Science,* May 20, 1966, p. 1032ff.

49. Boyer, "New Ties that Bind SUNY." *Educom,* April 1966, p. 1.

50. The New York *Times,* March 5, 1965, p. 1.

51. Kaplan, "An Unhurried View of Copyright: Proposals and Prospects." *Columbia Law Review,* May 1965, p. 851-852.

52. *Library Journal,* August 1966, p. 3672.

53. *Bulletin of the Copyright Society of the U.S.A.*, August 1964, p. 369ff.

54. *M.U.L.L.* (Modern Uses of Logic in Law), June 1965, p. 44ff.

55. Supplementary Report of the Register of Copyright on the General Revision of the U.S. Copyright Law: 1965 Revision Bill, p. 20.

56. Kaplan, *op. cit.*, p. 843-844.

57. U.S. *Congress, House, op. cit.*, p. 1459-1460.

Persons Interviewed and Consulted

Asleson, Robert F., senior vice president–operations, University Microfilms Inc., Ann Arbor, Mich.

Barad, Elizabeth, legal counsel, Random House, New York, N.Y.

Barnard, J. Darrell, professor of science education, New York University.

Barnes, Donald E., vice president, Institute for Educational Development, New York, N.Y.

Barstow, Merton C., assistant director, Office of Research Contracts, Harvard University.

Bates, Emmert W., vice president, American Book Co., New York, N.Y.

Baum, Werner A., vice president for scientific affairs, New York University.

Benjamin, Curtis G., chairman of the board, McGraw-Hill Book Co., New York, N.Y.

Bright, R. Louis, Associate Commissioner for Research, U.S. Office of Education, Washington, D.C.

Buss, William G., assistant to the dean, Graduate School of Education, Harvard University.

Cunningham, Dewey J., manager of patent services, IBM, Armonk, N.Y.

Deighton, Lee C., chairman of the board, Macmillan Co., New York, N.Y.

Derenberg, Walter E., professor of law, New York University.

Dershimer, Richard A., executive officer, American Educational Research Association, Washington, D.C.

Ferman, Louis, research director, Institute of Labor and Industrial Relations, University of Michigan.

Finkelstein, Herman N., attorney; general counsel, ASCAP, New York, N.Y.

Fisher, John H., professor of English, New York University; executive secretary, Modern Language Association of America; editor, PMLA.

Frase, Robert W., director of the Joint Washington office of American Book Publishers Council and the American Textbook Publishers Institute, Washington, D.C.

Goldberg, Morton D., chairman, Copyright Division of the American Bar Association's Patent, Trademark, and Copyright Section; secretary, Copyright Society of America, Washington, D.C.

Goldman, Abraham, general counsel, Register of Copyrights, Washington, D.C.

Gordon, Ben, clerk, U.S. Senate Small Business Committee, Washington, D.C.

Goren, Arnold L., professor of education, New York University.

Gosnell, Charles F., director of libraries, New York University.

Griffiths, Daniel, dean, School of Education, New York University.

Hagel, Raymond C., president and chairman of the board, Crowell Collier and Macmillan, Inc., New York, N.Y.

Harvey, William B., director, New York University Press.

Harvith, Bernard Evans, professor of law, Albany Law School, Union University.

Hattery, Lowell H., professor of law and government administration, American University.

Hayes, Robert M., director, Institute of Library Research, University of California, Los Angeles.

Hoff, J. W., general counsel, National Science Foundation, Washington, D.C.

Holton, Gerald J., professor of physics, Harvard University.

Hoppenfeld, Ellias C., president, Law Research Service, Inc., New York, N.Y.

Horty, John F., professor of law, University of Pittsburgh; chairman, ABA Special Committee on Electronic Data Retrieval.

Howe, II, Harold, U.S. Commissioner of Education, Washington, D.C.

Kaelber, Edward G., associate dean, Graduate School of Education, Harvard University.

Kaminstein, Abraham L., Register of Copyrights, Washington, D.C.

Karp, Irwin, legal counsel, Authors League of America, Inc., New York, N.Y.

Keppel, Francis, chairman, General Learning Corp., New York, N.Y.

Lacy, Dan M., managing director, American Book Publishers Council, Inc., New York, N.Y.

Linden, Bella L., attorney, New York, N.Y.

Lindsey, Wendell, legislative assistant to U.S. Senator Russell B. Long (La.), Washington, D.C.

Martin, Lowell A., vice president and executive director, The Grolier Society, Inc., New York, N.Y.

McCaffrey, Austin J., executive director, American Textbook Publishers Institute, New York, N.Y.

Melcher, Daniel, president, R. R. Bowker Co., New York, N.Y.

Mitchell, Stephen A., attorney, Chicago, Ill.

Morse, Jack, head, legislative division, American Council on Education, Washington, D.C.

Mylecraine, Walter E., special assistant to the Deputy Commissioner of Education, U.S. Office of Education, Washington, D.C.

Newmann, Fred M., assistant professor of education, Harvard University.

Power, Eugene B., chairman, University Microfilms, Inc., Ann Arbor, Mich.

Riecken, Henry W., associate director of science education, National Science Foundation, Washington, D.C.

Roth, Sidney, director, Office of Research, New York University.

Rutherford, F. James, assistant professor of education, Harvard University.

Samuels, Norvell B., president, American Book Co., New York, N.Y.

Schnapper, M. B., editor and publisher, Public Affairs Press, New York, N.Y.

Schulman, John, attorney, New York, N.Y.

Serviss, Trevor, K., vice president and chairman of editorial committee, L. W. Singer Co., Inc., New York, N.Y.

Shugg, Roger W., director, University of Chicago Press.

Sizer, Theodore R., dean, Graduate School of Education, Harvard University.

Spaulding, William E., president, Houghton, Mifflin Co., Boston, Mass.

Steinberg Erwin R., dean, Margaret Morrison Carnegie College, Carnegie Institute of Technology.

Swett, Albert H., vice president and general counsel, Xerox Corp., Rochester, N.Y.

Waller, Theodore, president, Teaching Materials Corp., New York, N.Y.

Wessell, Nils Y., president, Institute for Educational Development, New York, N.Y.

Wigren, Harold E., chairman of the *Ad Hoc* Committee (of Educational Institutions and Organizations) on Copyright Law Revision, Washington, D.C.; associate director of NEA's Division of Audiovisual Instructional Service.

Wiley, William Bradford, president, John Wiley & Sons., Inc., New York, N.Y.

Wilson, John T., deputy director, National Science Foundation, Washington, D.C.

The Fund for the Advancement of Education

is a philanthropic organization established in 1951 by the Ford Foundation to work in the field of formal education. Its chief activity is the support of experimental programs that hold promise of advancing education in American schools and colleges. To date the Fund has been granted approximately $72 million by the Ford Foundation.